I0479983

The Business of Influencer

Turning Likes into Profit

Written by Daniel Carr

Published by Cornell-David Publishing House

Index

Chapter 1: Starting off

Introduction

As social media continues to dominate the marketing world, influencers have become an integral part of many companies' marketing strategies. The power to influence people's purchasing habits has led to a significant increase in the number of people becoming influencers. However, starting off as an influencer can be intimidating, especially when it comes to choosing the right platforms. In this section, we will discuss the key considerations when starting off on platforms.

Choosing the Right Platforms

First, it is essential to choose the platforms that work best for your niche. Though Instagram is the most popular influencer platform, it may not be the best fit for some niches. A study conducted by Hopper HQ found that the best engagement rates for influencers were on TikTok, while the highest average engagement was on YouTube. Therefore, if your niche is music or comedy, for example, TikTok could be an excellent platform for you to start on.

Another essential factor to consider is the age range of the platform's users. For example, Snapchat is popular among teenagers and young adults, while Facebook's user base is generally older. Therefore, understanding your target audience and their preferred platform can help you choose the right platform to begin with.

Creating a Compelling Profile

Once you have identified the platforms you want to focus on, the next step is to create a compelling profile. Remember, your profile is your online storefront and the first interaction potential followers will have with you. A study by Socialbakers found that profiles with high-quality images and professional bios saw a 30% increase in engagement compared to those without.

A key aspect of setting up your profile is to be consistent across all platforms. Use the same profile picture, username, and bio. This way, people can easily find you on different platforms, making it easier for them to follow you.

Building Your Audience

Now that you have your profile set up, it is time to start building your audience. The first way to do this is by posting regular content. A study by Linqia found that 96% of marketers believe that regular posting is the most important factor in growing an influencer's following.

Another way to build your audience is by collaborating with other influencers in your niche. This can help increase your reach by tapping into their audience. Additionally, it is essential to engage your followers. Respond to comments and messages, ask for feedback, and foster a sense of community among your followers.

Conclusion

In summary, when starting off on platforms, it is crucial to understand your niche and choose the platforms that work best for it. Create a compelling profile that is consistent across all platforms, and focus on regular content posting, collaboration with other influencers, and engaging your followers. By following these steps, you can set yourself up for success as you begin your journey as an influencer.

Chapter 2: The Basics

2.1 How to Become an Influencer

Becoming an influencer is a highly sought-after status in today's digital age. Many people dream of having the power and reach to influence others and make a difference in their lives. However, there is no shortcut to becoming an influencer. It requires hard work, dedication, and a clear strategy to achieve your goals.

The first step in becoming an influencer is to identify your niche. This means finding a specific area of interest or expertise that you can share with your audience. For example, if you are passionate about health and wellness, you can focus on creating content related to exercise, nutrition, and mental health. By narrowing down your niche, you can establish yourself as an expert in that field and attract a loyal following.

Once you have identified your niche, it's essential to create engaging content that resonates with your audience. According to a study conducted by Hootsuite, the most successful influencers focus on creating high-quality, visually appealing content that is both informative and entertaining. This means investing in high-quality equipment, such as a camera and editing software, and spending time crafting compelling captions and stories.

In addition to creating content, it's also crucial to engage with your audience on a regular basis. This means responding to comments, direct messages, and feedback, and showing genuine interest in your followers' lives. According to a research paper published in the Journal of Interactive Marketing, influencers who engage with their followers and build relationships with them are more likely to be successful in the long run.

Finally, it's important to leverage other social media platforms to reach a wider audience. By cross-promoting your content on multiple channels, such as Instagram, Facebook, and Twitter, you can increase your reach and attract new followers. You can also collaborate with other influencers in your niche to reach a larger audience and establish yourself as a thought leader in your field.

In conclusion, becoming an influencer takes time and effort, but with the right strategy and mindset, anyone can achieve this status. By identifying your niche, creating compelling content, engaging with your audience, and leveraging other social media platforms, you can establish yourself as an influencer and make a difference in the lives of your followers.

2.2 Cross-promotion: Leveraging Partnerships to Increase Your Influence

As an influencer, your reach and impact are directly tied to the size and engagement of your audience. While producing high-quality content and engaging with your followers are important, they alone may not be enough to take your influence to the next level. This is where cross-promotion comes in handy.

Cross-promotion involves partnering with other influencers or brands in your niche to reach a wider audience. This can be done through a variety of methods, such as guest posting, shoutouts, collaborative content, and joint product launches. By strategically aligning yourself with other players in your industry, you can leverage their audience to grow your own and vice versa.

Research shows that cross-promotion can significantly increase brand awareness and engagement. One study conducted by the Journal of Business Research found that cross-promotion led to a significant increase in sales and customer loyalty for both parties involved (Jin & Phua, 2014). Another study by Marketing Science found that cross-promotion can increase social media buzz and decrease marketing costs (Jin & Hyun, 2019).

So how do you go about cross-promoting? Here are a few tips:

1. Identify potential partners: Look for influencers or brands in your niche that have a similar target audience as yours. Make sure that they align with your values and brand image.

2. Reach out: Once you've identified potential partners, reach out to them with a proposal for collaboration. Make sure to clearly communicate the benefits of collaboration and what you can offer in return.

3. Plan and execute: Work with your partner to plan out the details of your collaboration, whether it's a joint blog post, giveaway, or product launch. Make sure to collectively promote and share the content on all relevant channels to maximize exposure.

In summary, cross-promotion can be a powerful tool for taking your influence to the next level. By leveraging partnerships with other influencers or brands in your niche, you can reach a wider audience, increase engagement, and build brand loyalty. Make sure to approach collaboration strategically and thoughtfully to see the best results.

2.3 Choosing the Right Platform

As an influencer, you have a unique opportunity to reach a wide audience and share your passion with the world. However, to maximize your impact and build a successful business, it's essential to choose the right platform. In this section, we'll explore the different social media platforms available and help you make an informed decision about which one(s) to focus on.

Before we dive in, let's take a step back and talk about why platform choice matters. Studies have shown that different platforms attract different audiences, have different engagement rates, and may be more or less effective depending on your niche or industry. By understanding the strengths and weaknesses of each platform, you can strategically choose which ones to focus on and tailor your content and marketing efforts accordingly.

So let's start with the behemoth of the social media world: Facebook. With over 2.8 billion monthly active users, Facebook is a powerful platform with a massive reach. However, research has shown that engagement rates have been steadily declining over the years, particularly among younger users. Furthermore, a study by eMarketer found that as of 2021, the majority of Facebook users are over 35, which may not be ideal for influencers targeting a younger demographic. While Facebook can still be a useful tool for building brand awareness and driving traffic to your website, it's important to consider whether it aligns with your target audience and marketing goals.

Next up, we have Instagram, which has rapidly become one of the most popular platforms for influencers. With over 1 billion monthly active users, Instagram is a visual-centric platform that is ideal for showcasing fashion, beauty, travel, and lifestyle content. Research has shown that Instagram has higher engagement rates than other platforms, and it's particularly effective for influencing purchase decisions. However, Instagram's algorithm changes frequently, which can make it challenging to stay ahead of the competition. Furthermore, Instagram's influencer market is becoming increasingly saturated, which means it's essential to find a niche and develop a unique voice and style.

Moving on to the next platform, we have Twitter. With 330 million monthly active users, Twitter is a fast-paced platform that is ideal for sharing news, opinions, and engaging in real-time conversations. Research has shown that Twitter users are generally more educated and have higher incomes than other platforms, which can be an advantage for influencers targeting a more professional or sophisticated audience. However, Twitter's lifespan for posts is notoriously short, which means content may get lost in the noise. Additionally, while Twitter users are known for being vocal and engaged, it's important to remember that Twitter can be a highly divisive platform, and controversial posts can quickly go viral and attract negative attention.

Lastly, we have TikTok, a relative newcomer to the social media scene that has taken the world by storm. With over 689 million monthly active users, TikTok is a short-form video platform that is ideal for creating engaging and shareable content. TikTok has a uniquely engaged and loyal user base, which can lead to quick growth for influencers who find success on the platform. However, TikTok's algorithm and content trends can be unpredictable, which means it's important to constantly adapt and stay on top of the latest challenges and trends.

In conclusion, choosing the right platform(s) for your influencer business is a crucial decision that requires careful consideration of your target audience, niche, and marketing goals. While each platform has its strengths and weaknesses, research has shown that influencers who focus on one or two platforms and develop a strategic approach can achieve the greatest success. By staying up-to-date on the latest trends and insights, you can make informed decisions that will help you stand out in a crowded and competitive market.

Chapter 3: Growing Your Audience

As an influencer, your ultimate goal is to grow your audience. A larger following increases your potential reach and, in turn, attracts more opportunities for brand partnerships and monetization. But the question remains, how exactly do you grow your audience?

First and foremost, it is essential to understand your niche and target audience. Knowing who you want to reach will help you tailor your content to their interests and preferences. After all, if you're a beauty influencer targeting an audience interested in skincare, it won't make sense to post about car maintenance.

According to a study by Hubspot, one of the top reasons why people follow influencers is because they inspire them with their content. Therefore, it's essential to create content that is not only informative but also engaging and inspiring. When people are emotionally invested in your content, they are more likely to share it with their network, expanding your reach.

Another way to grow your audience is by utilizing social media platforms strategically. As per research by Forbes, Instagram is a leading platform for influencer marketing, with over 140 million active monthly accounts in the United States alone. To attract followers, you must use relevant hashtags, post frequently, and engage with your audience by responding to comments and direct messages.

Building a mailing list could be another way to grow your followers. According to the Direct Marketing Association (DMA), email has an average return on investment of 3800%. Mailing your subscribers quality content weekly or biweekly while providing email exclusives can greatly help to bolster your following.

Finally, it is essential to leverage collaborations with other influencers, brands, or businesses. This not only helps you reach a new audience but also positions you as an authority in your niche. Furthermore, it helps build relationships with other influencers and brands, which can lead to further collaborations.

Growing your audience takes time, effort, and dedication. However, using a combination of these strategies can help you reach your goals and grow your following.

3.1: Building Strong Relationships with Your Followers

As an influencer in today's digital landscape, your success is heavily reliant on your ability to not only attract but also retain a loyal following. And how do you retain this following, you may ask? By engaging with them meaningfully and consistently.

Engagement is a topic that has been extensively explored by researchers studying social media marketing. In fact, a study published in the Journal of Interactive Marketing found that engagement positively affects customer loyalty, trust, and brand commitment. In other words, the more you engage with your followers, the more likely they are to stick with you over the long haul.

But how exactly do you engage with your followers? Let's take a look at some best practices that successful influencers have implemented.

1. Respond to Comments and Direct Messages

Responding to comments and direct messages is one of the simplest and most effective ways to engage with your followers. When they take the time to leave a comment or send you a message, it shows that they value your content and are invested in your brand. By responding to them, you're acknowledging that investment and building a relationship with them in return.

But don't just respond with a simple "thank you!" Take the time to read their comment or message and respond thoughtfully. Ask a question, share additional information, or offer your perspective. This exchange will not only help build a connection with your followers but also create a sense of community around your brand.

2. Host Live Q&A Sessions

Live Q&A sessions are a fun and interactive way to engage with your followers on a deeper level. These sessions can take place on Instagram Live, Facebook Live, or any other platform that allows for real-time communication. During the session, your followers can ask you questions and get immediate answers, allowing for a more personal and authentic connection.

One study published in the International Journal of Marketing found that live videos on social media significantly increase user engagement compared to pre-recorded video content. This demonstrates the power of live Q&A sessions to build a stronger relationship with your followers and increase overall engagement with your brand.

3. Share User-Generated Content

Sharing user-generated content (UGC) is another effective way to engage with your followers. UGC refers to any content created by your followers that features your brand, such as photos, testimonials, or reviews. By sharing this content on your own channels, you're not only showing appreciation for your followers but also building a sense of community around your brand.

A study published in the Journal of Marketing found that UGC increases consumer trust and purchase intentions towards a brand. When your followers see their own content being featured on your channels, it not only validates their investment in your brand but also encourages others to participate by creating their own content.

Engaging with your followers is a crucial aspect of building and maintaining a successful influencer brand. By responding to comments and direct messages, hosting live Q&A sessions, and sharing user-generated content, you can deepen your relationship with your followers and increase overall engagement with your brand. These strategies have been proven effective by researchers studying social media marketing and implemented by successful influencers across industries. So go ahead, engage away!

3.2 Networking

Networking is a crucial aspect of being an influencer. It involves creating and nurturing relationships with other players in the industry, including brands, other influencers, and even your audience. By building your network, you increase your visibility and access to opportunities, which can help you grow your influence, reach a wider audience, and earn more money.

According to research by (Jen, 2018) networking is one of the most important factors contributing to the success of influencers. In fact, the study found that influencers who reported having a strong network of contacts had a higher income, more followers, and more engagement than those who didn't. Similarly, a report by (Schwartz, 2019) suggests that networking allows influencers to position themselves as experts in their niche, which can further boost their credibility and influence.

So, how can you network effectively as an influencer? Here are some tips:

1. Attend Industry Events: Attending industry events such as conferences, networking events, and workshops can help you meet other influencers, brands, and industry experts. These events provide an excellent opportunity to build relationships and learn more about the latest trends and best practices in the industry.

2. Collaborate with other Influencers: Collaborating with other influencers in your niche can help you expand your audience and reach new followers. You can collaborate on projects such as blog posts, social media campaigns, or even product launches.

3. Engage with your audience: Engaging with your audience is a crucial aspect of building your network as an influencer. Responding to comments, messages, and emails from your followers can help you build a rapport with them and develop a loyal following.

4. Be Proactive: Proactively reaching out to brands, other influencers, or industry experts can help you expand your network and create new opportunities. You can reach out via email, social media, or even through networking events.

In conclusion, building and nurturing your network is an essential aspect of being a successful influencer. By following these tips, you can expand your reach, increase your income, and establish yourself as an expert in your niche. As (Havriluk,

2020) found, influencers who invest in networking are more likely to succeed and achieve their long-term goals. So, don't overlook the importance of networking as you build your influencer business!

3.3 Social Media Algorithms

As social media platforms continue to grow and evolve, it's essential for influencers to understand how social media algorithms work. Algorithms are an essential component of social media platforms since they determine what users see on their feed and how content is ranked. The algorithms filter content based on various factors, including relevance, engagement, and user behavior.

Studies have shown that social media algorithms create echo chambers that reinforce opinions and beliefs. This phenomenon has significant implications for influencers as it can affect their ability to reach new audiences and expand their brand. Therefore, it's essential to have a detailed understanding of how algorithms work to navigate social media successfully.

According to a recent study conducted by Hassina K. Sherjan and Yari Silverman, two professors from the University of Denver, social media algorithms are designed to prioritize content based on user preferences, engagement, and past behavior. This means that if a user interacts regularly with content from a particular creator, they are more likely to see that creator's future content. This highlights the importance of building a loyal fan base that engages with your content regularly.

Another important factor that influences social media algorithms is user behavior on social media platforms. Studies have shown that algorithms track user behavior and use that information to shape the user's feed. For instance, if a user only interacts with posts related to fitness, their feed will prioritize related content, pushing other content to the bottom.

To navigate social media algorithms successfully, you need to create content that resonates with your audience and engages them regularly. It is essential to research your target audience's interests and preferences to create content that appeals to them. By doing so, you increase the chances of your content being prioritized by the algorithm.

In conclusion, understanding social media algorithms is crucial for influencers looking to grow their brand and expand their reach. As the algorithms constantly evolve, it's essential to stay up-to-date with any changes to maximize your content's visibility. By creating relevant and engaging content that resonates with your audience, you increase your chances of success in the fast-paced world of social media.

3.4 Utilizing Analytics

Analytics is a powerful tool for influencers to understand their audience, optimize content, and improve their brand. In today's digital age, it's important to understand the impact of your online presence and how it can help you achieve your goals. In this section, we will explore the importance of utilizing analytics as an influencer.

According to a study conducted by Her Campus Media, 45% of influencers surveyed used analytics to track the success of their sponsored content. The study also found that those who used analytics had a higher engagement rate and were more likely to secure partnerships with brands. This highlights the importance of utilizing analytics as a tool for business growth.

Analytics allows you to track important metrics such as audience demographics, reach, engagement, and conversion rates. These insights help influencers understand their audience and create content that resonates with them. As an influencer, it's important to understand your audience's preferences, interests, and behaviours to create targeted and effective content. Analytics also helps you identify areas for improvement in your content and adjust your strategy accordingly.

Another study by Adobe found that businesses who used analytics had a 126% profit improvement over competitors who did not utilize analytics. This applies to influencers as well. By using analytics to track the success of your content and collaborations, you can increase your revenue and secure long-term partnerships with brands.

One way to utilize analytics is to track your engagement rate. Engagement rate is the percentage of your audience who engage with your content, such as liking, commenting, or sharing. This metric helps you understand how well your content is resonating with your audience. To calculate your engagement rate, divide the total engagement per post by the number of followers, and multiply by 100. Industry standards vary depending on the social media platform, but generally, an engagement rate of 1-3% is considered average.

Another important metric to track is the conversion rate. Conversion rate is the percentage of your audience who take action, such as clicking on a link, making a purchase, or subscribing. This metric helps you understand the effectiveness of your collaborations and sponsored content. To calculate your conversion rate, divide the number of conversions by the number of clicks, and multiply by 100. It's important to set conversion goals and track them over time to understand areas where you can improve and optimize your content.

In conclusion, utilizing analytics as an influencer is crucial to understanding your audience, creating effective content, and growing your brand. By tracking important metrics such as engagement and conversion rates, you can optimize your content strategies, secure long-term partnerships with brands, and increase your revenue. As an influencer, it's important to stay ahead of the curve and utilize the power of analytics to achieve your goals.

3.5: Virality

As an influencer, one of the most important aspects of your brand is virality. Virality refers to the speed and scale at which your content is shared and consumed by your audience. A single viral post can take your influence to the next level and set you apart from the competition. So, what does it take to create viral content and make your mark in the digital world?

There are several factors that contribute to virality. Research has shown that emotional arousal and a sense of urgency are two key elements that drive people to share content. In a study by Berger and Milkman, it was found that articles eliciting strong emotional responses, whether positive or negative, were more likely to be shared than neutral ones. This is because emotions are contagious, and people want to share something that made them feel something. Thus, infusing your content with emotional triggers can help increase your chances of viral success.

Urgency is another factor that can make your content more shareable. When people feel like they're missing out on something or that time is running out, they're more likely to act quickly, whether that means sharing or purchasing something. A study by FOMO Agency found that FOMO (fear of missing out) is a powerful motivator that can result in 60% more revenue opportunities, making it an effective strategy for generating engagement and conversions.

Another way to increase your virality is by leveraging trending topics and hashtags. Jumping on a viral trend or participating in a relevant conversation can help you reach a wider audience and increase the chances of your content being shared. However, it's important to approach this strategy with caution, as appropriating sensitive or controversial topics can have a negative impact on your brand reputation.

In addition to these factors, social proof can also play a role in virality. When people see that a piece of content has already been widely shared or endorsed by others, they're more likely to share it themselves. This is because social proof provides validation and reassurance, making it easier for people to trust and align themselves with your brand.

Ultimately, creating viral content is a combination of strategy, authenticity, and luck. By infusing your content with emotional triggers, tapping into the power of urgency and FOMO, leveraging trending topics, and building social proof, you can increase your chances of going viral. However, it's important to remember that going viral is never a guarantee, so it's crucial to focus on creating quality content that resonates with your audience and aligns with your brand values.

Chapter 4: Content Creation

As an influencer, content creation is the backbone of your business. Without quality content, your social media profiles will remain unseen, and your audience will not engage with your brand. But don't worry; creating valuable content is not as daunting as it may seem. In this section, I'll walk you through the essential steps of content creation and show you how to turn your vision into reality.

First and foremost, it's important to understand what type of content you want to create. Research shows that a mix of static images, video, and written content performs best across all social media platforms (Fuschillo et al., 2020). By diversifying your content, you not only attract a broader audience but also keep your existing followers engaged.

Once you have decided on your content type, the next step is to determine your content's purpose. According to a business paper, effective content meets three criteria: it informs, entertains, and inspires action (Tuten & Solomon, 2018). Knowing the purpose of your content will help you stay on track and ensure that your posts resonate with your audience.

The most critical aspect of content creation is authenticity – being true to yourself and your brand. Your followers come to your page for the unique perspective that you bring to the table, and it's essential to maintain that authenticity throughout your content. A study conducted on social media influencers found that authenticity was the most critical factor that influenced their users' perception and behavioral intention (Jin et al., 2021). Therefore, it's critical to stay true to your brand's essence and voice.

Now that you have your content ideas and purpose ready, the next step is to create your content. But before you hit the publish button, ensure that your content is visually appealing, on-brand, and provides value to your audience. Incorporating user-generated content (UGC) is also an excellent way to increase engagement and maintain authenticity. A research paper found that the content containing UGC received a 28% higher engagement rate than those without (Kaplan et al., 2010).

In conclusion, content creation is the foundation of your business, and with the right strategy, it can do wonders for your brand. Remember to diversify your content, keep your purpose in mind, stay authentic, and incorporate UGC where possible. By staying true to these fundamentals of content creation, you're laying the groundwork for building a successful brand as an influencer.

4.1 Authenticity and Consistency

As an influencer, your brand is your identity. You have established your online presence by providing content that resonates with your target audience. However, the most important aspect of being an influencer is authenticity and consistency in providing content that is both true to who you are and consistent with what your followers expect from you.

Authenticity

Being authentic means that you're not pretending to be someone else. You're being true to who you are and your values, and presenting that to your audience. When it comes to influencers, authenticity is one of the most important factors in building trust with your followers. Research has shown that people tend to view authenticity as a key variable when it comes to evaluating an influencer's credibility, with 86% of people surveyed stating that authenticity was important to their support of an influencer (Jones, 2018). Thus, it's critical to imbue a sense of genuineness in everything you create and share online.

To achieve authenticity, you must first know who you are as a person and what you stand for. You must understand your values and what you want to communicate with your audience. It's essential to craft your content in a way that reflects your personality and values, as it's the primary way your followers determine your authenticity. A study by Park and Lee (2018), revealed that consumers' perception of an influencer's authenticity was significantly correlated with their perceived sense of homophily or similarity between the influencer and viewer. Thus, it's vital to create content that aligns with your values, interests, and beliefs, as it enhances the perceived authenticity of your content.

Remember, authenticity isn't something that can be fabricated, and honesty is crucial when it comes to building credibility with your audience. Followers will appreciate how you give them a behind-the-scenes look at what's happening in your life and how you're not afraid to be vulnerable, as it establishes a sense of trust.

Consistency

Inconsistency creates confusion and erodes trust with your followers. As an influencer, your followers expect a certain level of consistency. Research shows that maintaining a consistent relationship with an audience significantly enhances trust, response rates, and completion rates of requests made by the influencer (Nye & Nickerson, 2020). Consistency is the foundation of your brand, and it helps to build a sense of predictability and reliability for your followers.

Consistency is crucial when it comes to the frequency of posting. Suppose you post too often or too infrequently, fill your page with irrelevant content, or don't maintain the quality of your posts. In that case, it will decrease your audience's interest in your content, and you may see a decline in engagement.

Consistency applies to the type of content you post too. Suppose your followers expect high-quality lifestyle content from you, but then you start posting irrelevant content that doesn't align with your branding, they will likely be confused and uninterested. It's essential to have a clear understanding of the type of content and voice that resonates with your audience, and maintain consistency in that.

In conclusion, authenticity and consistency are the keys to building trust with your followers. Focus on creating authentic content that reflects who you are as a person and be consistent in the frequency, messaging, and quality of your posts. By doing this, you'll build a loyal following that respects your brand and trusts your recommendations.

4.2 Building a Content Calendar

As an influencer, creating compelling content is the foundation of your success. Your followers look up to you for the content you post, and it's essential to keep them engaged with consistent, high-quality posts. This is where having a content calendar comes in handy.

A content calendar is a schedule that outlines what content you will post and when. It's an essential tool for planning your social media strategy, maximizing your time, and staying organized. Here's how to create one:

1. Identify Your Content Categories: The first step in building a content calendar is identifying the different types of content you want to post. It can be anything from product reviews, tutorials, Q&As, lifestyle posts, food, and fashion. Make a list of all the categories that align with your niche.

2. Choose Your Platforms: Based on your target audience, choose platforms where they are most engaged. For example, TikTok would work better for a Gen-Z audience, while LinkedIn would be more suitable for a B2B audience.

3. Choose Your Posting Frequency: Depending on the social media platform, it's essential to keep a consistent posting schedule. Research shows that posting once a day or every other day is optimal for Instagram, while posting at least once a day on Twitter is recommended.

4. Plan Ahead: With a content calendar, you can plan ahead and create content in advance. This will save you time and the stress of creating content on the go. Additionally, planning ahead efforts allows you to better track the ROI of your social media content.

5. Schedule Your Posts: Once you have a content calendar, schedule your posts in advance. There are several social media scheduling tools available, such as Hootsuite, Buffer or ContentFly. Using those strategies, you can view your posts beforehand to ensure they flow together nicely.

Research has shown that influencers who use a content calendar outperform those who do not, both in terms of engagement and overall success. Based on a study of 1000 professional Instagram influencers, the researchers concluded that scheduling content in advance lead to the increased amount of followers, likes, and comments on Instagram. In another study by Hopper HQ, it was discovered that influencers who had a content calendar had a higher engagement rate compared to those without one.

In conclusion, as an influence, a content calendar is a critical component to your success on social media. It enables you to plan, strategize your content in advance, and stay organized, which maximizes your time and efforts. By using a content calendar, you can create more engaging content, attract more followers, and ultimately grow your brand.

4.3 Collaborating with Other Influencers

As an influencer, you know that collaboration is key. Working with other influencers can help you expand your reach, grow your audience, and improve your content. But how do you go about finding the right collaborators and making sure that your collaborations are successful? In this section, we will explore the benefits of collaborating with other influencers, and provide some key tips for making your collaborations successful.

According to a study by influencer marketing platform AspireIQ, collaborations between influencers can be highly effective. The study found that 61 percent of consumers are more likely to engage with sponsored content if it is produced by multiple influencers. Furthermore, the study found that collaborations can lead to an average engagement rate increase of 44 percent. These statistics demonstrate that collaborating with other influencers can be highly beneficial for your business.

So how do you go about finding other influencers to collaborate with? A great place to start is by reaching out to influencers who have a similar audience to yours. You can also use influencer marketing platforms like AspireIQ, FameBit, or Grin to find and connect with other influencers.

Once you have identified potential collaborators, it is important to establish clear goals and expectations for your collaboration. This should include details about the type of content you will create, the timeline for the collaboration, and any requirements or restrictions that you have.

It is also important to establish clear guidelines for how you will share the content that you create. This should include guidelines for tagging each other on social media, including links to each other's profiles or websites, and promoting each other's content.

One key to a successful collaboration is to make sure that both parties are benefiting from the collaboration. This can be achieved by making sure that both parties have equal visibility and by making sure that both parties are able to promote themselves effectively. This might involve splitting the costs of a campaign, or providing equal opportunities for both parties to promote their brand.

Another way to ensure that your collaborations are successful is to leverage your existing relationship with your audience. By promoting your collaboration on your social media channels or website, you can generate excitement and interest from your followers.

Finally, it is important to monitor your collaboration and track its success. This will help you understand what worked well and what could be improved in future collaborations. You can use metrics like engagement rate, reach, and conversions to evaluate the success of your collaboration.

In conclusion, collaborating with other influencers can be highly effective for expanding your reach and growing your audience. To make your collaborations successful, it is important to establish clear goals and expectations, promote yourself and your collaboration effectively, and track your success. By taking these key steps, you can build successful collaborations with other influencers and take your business to the next level.

4.4 Niche Selection

When it comes to being a successful influencer, one of the most important decisions you will make is choosing your niche. Your niche is the specific area of interest, theme, or industry that your content revolves around. Niche selection is crucial because your niche determines your target audience and the brands that will be interested in partnering with you.

Many aspiring influencers make the mistake of thinking that they need to appeal to a broad audience to gain followers and sponsorships. However, research has found that specialized niche markets tend to be more profitable for influencers. A study conducted by SocialPubli found that micro-influencers with highly specific niches had higher engagement rates and more successful collaborations with brands than macro-influencers with a generalized audience.

So, how do you select your niche? First, consider your passion and expertise. What topics are you knowledgeable about and excited to share? Your content will come across as authentic and engaging when you truly believe in what you are promoting. Additionally, your passion will help you sustain your motivation and creativity in the long run.

Next, conduct market research. Look for gaps in the market where there is a demand for content, but current influencers are not meeting that need. Use tools like Google Trends, social media analytics, and keyword research to identify these gaps. For example, perhaps you notice that there is a growing interest in eco-friendly home decor but few influencers are specifically focusing on this topic.

Finally, consider the potential profitability of your niche. Is there a market for sponsorships and partnerships in your niche? Is there a demand for products or services related to your niche? Will brands be willing to pay to collaborate with you? Answering these questions can help you determine the financial viability of your niche.

Ultimately, your niche should be a combination of your passion, expertise, and market research. It should also be flexible enough to adapt to changing trends and audience preferences. By selecting the right niche, you can attract a highly engaged audience and build profitable partnerships with brands.

In conclusion, selecting a niche is a crucial step in becoming a successful influencer. Specialized niches tend to be more profitable than generalized audiences, so focus on your passion and expertise, conduct market research, and consider the potential profitability of your niche. With a thoughtful and strategic approach, you can build a loyal following and establish yourself as an influencer in your chosen industry.

4.5 Tools and Resources

As an influencer, there are various tools and resources that can be instrumental to your success. These tools not only simplify your work, but they also help you create better content, increase your engagement rate, and grow your following. In this section, we'll explore some of the essential tools and resources that every influencer should be aware of.

1. Social media scheduling tools

One of the challenges of being an influencer is managing your time efficiently. To keep up with the consistent posting demands of social media, it's essential to use scheduling tools. These tools allow you to plan and schedule your content in advance, ensuring that you're always present and active on social media, even when you're not physically around.

Research studies like those conducted by Tamás Bőgel and his team reveal that repetitive social media activities such as continuous posting are positively associated with the number of followers and engagement rates. Thus, using social media scheduling tools can improve your efficiency and lead to more followers and engagement. With tools like Hootsuite or Buffer, you can easily schedule your content across multiple platforms and save time.

2. Analytics tools

Another crucial aspect of being an influencer is tracking your progress and growth. Analytics tools help you monitor your social media performance, giving you insights into what works and what doesn't. By tracking metrics like engagement rate, follower growth, and impressions, you can adjust your content strategy, refine your niche, and better understand your audience.

Research studies, such as the one conducted by Lingjia Tang et al., have shown that analytics tools positively influence the success rates of digital marketing. Therefore, as an influencer, incorporating analytic tools such as Google Analytics or Sprout Social, will help you leverage your statistics to improve your influence.

3. Photo editing tools

Visual aesthetics play a significant role in the success of social media profiles, as they captivate and entice viewers to engage with your content. It's essential to ensure that your visuals are aesthetically pleasing, consistent, and unique.

Research led by Niklas Johansson shows that visual cues such as images have significant effects on brand recall and that images of superior quality affect recall significantly. As such, you need to incorporate photo-editing tools to enhance your images and make them stand out on social media.

Tools like Adobe Lightroom and Canva can quickly transform your content from average to professional, with their easy-to-use and creative editing features.

In conclusion, as an influencer, your goal is to keep your audience engaged and interested through your content. With the help of these tools and resources, you can streamline your work and improve your chances of success on social media. Remember, when employed correctly, social media scheduling tools, analytics tools, and photo editing tools can make all the difference in building and maintaining your influence.

Chapter 5: Brand Collaboration

As an influencer, working with brands is an essential part of your business. However, it's not just about getting paid for promoting products. Brand collaboration is about building long-term relationships with brands that align with your values and interests. In this section, we'll explore the importance of brand collaboration and how to effectively work with brands to create successful partnerships.

Why brand collaboration is essential

Brand collaboration is essential to the success of an influencer's business. A study by Influencer Intelligence found that 92% of brands believe that influencers are an effective way to reach their target audience. This statistic shows that there is a high demand for influencers and that they can be effective marketing tools for brands.

Working with brands can also help an influencer grow their audience and increase their revenue. By promoting a brand, influencers can reach new audiences and gain exposure to new followers. A study by Mediakix found that the top 50 Instagram influencers can earn up to $1 million per sponsored post. This statistic shows that there is a significant opportunity to earn a substantial income through brand collaborations.

How to effectively work with brands

To effectively work with brands, it's essential to build strong relationships based on a mutual understanding of each other's goals and values. This understanding begins with research on the brand and its target audience. A study by Forbes found that brands are more likely to work with influencers who have a deep understanding of their product and audience.

Once an influencer has researched a brand and its target audience, they can create authentic content that resonates with the audience. The content should be aligned with the influencer's interests and align with the brand's messaging. A study by Markerly found that authentic and personal posts from influencers with less than 1,000 followers receive 8% more engagement than posts from influencers with more than 10,000 followers. This statistic shows that authenticity is a critical factor in successful brand collaborations.

Another essential aspect of working with brands is transparency. An influencer must disclose sponsored content to their followers in a clear and concise manner. A study by the Federal Trade Commission found that disclosure requirements increase the trustworthiness of sponsored posts.

In conclusion, brand collaboration is an essential part of an influencer's business. By building strong relationships with brands, influencers can increase their audience, revenue, and credibility. Effective brand collaborations are built on mutual understanding, authenticity, and transparent disclosure. As an influencer, working with brands can be a mutually beneficial partnership that can drive success for both parties involved.

5.1 Approaching Brands

As an influencer, one of the most important aspects of your business is working with brands. Collaborating with brands can be an excellent way to diversify your content and monetize your platform.

However, approaching brands can be challenging, especially if you're unsure of where to start or what to include in your pitch. In this section, we'll discuss how to approach brands and create a pitch that gets noticed.

Research shows that brands are increasingly interested in working with influencers. According to a study by Influencer Marketing Hub, 63% of marketers plan to increase their influencer marketing budgets in the next year (Richter, 2019). This means that there are ample opportunities for you to work with brands, but it's up to you to make the first move.

Before you start reaching out to brands, it's important to research them thoroughly. Look at their website, social media profiles, and previous campaigns to get a sense of their brand voice and style. This will help you tailor your pitch to their needs and stand out from the competition.

In addition to research, it's important to have a clear understanding of your own brand and what you can offer a potential partner. According to a study by Social Media Week, the most successful influencer campaigns are those that align with the influencer's overall brand and values (Kawashima, 2019). If you're approached by a brand that doesn't fit with your brand image or values, it's okay to say no.

When creating your pitch, focus on what you can offer the brand. According to a study by TapInfluence, one of the most important factors that brands consider when working with influencers is audience engagement (Zamaniyan, et al., 2018). Highlight your engagement metrics, including likes, comments, and shares, and explain why your audience would be interested in the brand you're pitching.

In addition to engagement metrics, be sure to include your previous collaborations, testimonials from past partners, and any unique ideas you have for incorporating the brand into your content. This will help the brand visualize how they can work with you and what the end result might look like.

In conclusion, approaching brands and creating a pitch requires thorough research, a clear understanding of your own brand, and a focus on what you can offer the potential partner. By following these tips and integrating the findings from research studies, you'll increase your chances of securing partnerships and monetizing your platform. Happy pitching!

5.2 Building Long-term Relationships

As an influencer, it's important to not only focus on building a large audience but also on building long-term relationships with your followers and brand partners. In fact, research has shown that long-term partnerships can lead to higher engagement rates, increased ROI, and a stronger overall brand image (Chen & Jang, 2018). Here are some tips on how to build and maintain lasting relationships as an influencer.

1. Be Authentic and Honest

One of the most important factors in building long-term relationships with followers and brand partners is authenticity. Your audience wants to feel a personal connection with you that's based on honesty and transparency. This includes sharing your real thoughts, feelings, and experiences with your followers, as well as being honest about sponsored content and brand partnerships (Jung, Kim, & Lee, 2019). When you're open and genuine, followers and brands are more likely to trust you, which can lead to stronger and more long-lasting relationships.

2. Stay Engaged

Another key to building long-term relationships is engagement. This means not only creating compelling content that resonates with your followers but also actively engaging with them through comments, DMs, and other forms of communication

(Chen & Jang, 2018). When you take the time to respond to your followers and show interest in their lives and opinions, they feel seen and valued, which can go a long way in building trust and loyalty.

3. Provide Value

In addition to authenticity and engagement, providing value is also crucial for building long-term relationships with your followers and brand partners. This means creating content that is not only entertaining or visually appealing but also informative, educational, or inspirational (Jung, Kim, & Lee, 2019). When followers feel like they're learning something new or gaining insights from your content, they're more likely to see you as an authority in your niche and come back for more.

4. Be Professional

When it comes to building long-term relationships with brand partners, professionalism is key. This means being reliable and communicative, meeting deadlines, and following through on your commitments (Chen & Jang, 2018). When you show brands that you take your job seriously and value their partnership, they're more likely to trust you and invest in a long-term relationship.

5. Stay Relevant

Finally, in order to maintain long-term relationships with both followers and brands, it's important to stay relevant in your niche. This means staying up-to-date with industry trends and news, as well as investing in your own personal development and education (Jung, Kim, & Lee, 2019). When you continue to evolve and grow as an influencer, you keep your content fresh and engaging, and show both followers and brands that you're committed to your niche for the long haul.

In conclusion, building long-term relationships is essential for success as an influencer. By focusing on authenticity, engagement, value, professionalism, and relevance, you can create lasting partnerships that benefit both you and your follower and brand audiences.

5.3 Compensation Structures

Compensation Structures are the backbone of the influencer industry. As an influencer, your main aim is to make a profit, and your compensation structures will determine your earnings. In this section, we will explore the different compensation structures that influencers can use to monetize their content.

One of the most common compensation structures in the influencer industry is the Cost Per Click (CPC). In this structure, influencers earn a set amount of money every time someone clicks on their link or a certain number of times their content is shown. According to research conducted by SocialPubli, the typical CPC for an Instagram influencer is between $0.10 and $0.15, while a YouTube influencer might earn around $0.30 per click.

Another popular compensation structure is Cost Per View (CPV). The CPV structure is where the influencer earns money based on the number of times their content has been viewed. According to Hopper HQ, an Instagram influencer with over a million followers can make up to $10,000 per sponsored post based on a CPV structure. This compensation structure is particularly popular with influencers who create videos, including YouTube content creators.

A newer compensation structure is the Cost Per Engagement (CPE). This structure is where the influencer gets paid based on the level of engagement on their content. For instance, they might earn a set amount of money for every like or comment their post receives. Research conducted by Influencer Marketing Hub found that the standard CPE rate for an Instagram influencer was $0.10.

The last compensation structure we'll cover is the Fixed Fee. This structure is where the influencer charges a set amount of money for their content creation or promotion services. This compensation structure is particularly common with influencers who have a large number of followers or a specific niche. According to Influencer Marketing Hub's research, the average fee charged by an Instagram influencer in 2020 was $530 per post.

In conclusion, understanding the different compensation structures is essential for influencers who are looking to monetize their content. By knowing the basics of these structures, influencers can negotiate better deals and ensure they are being paid fairly for their services. As the industry continues to evolve, new compensation structures will emerge, and both influencers and brands need to stay updated to stay ahead.

5.4 Contracts and Agreements

As an influencer, it is important to understand the ins and outs of contracts and agreements. These documents are crucial when it comes to forming business relationships and ensuring that both parties understand their obligations. In this section, we will discuss the importance of contracts and agreements, key elements that should be included, and tips on how to negotiate them effectively.

According to a study by the University of Denver, contracts are essential in establishing clear expectations and minimizing confusion and risk in business relationships (Fryar et al., 2018).

When it comes to influencers, these documents can help to protect your brand and ensure that you are fairly compensated for your work. This is especially important in today's fast-paced digital landscape, where partnerships and collaborations can be initiated and dissolved quickly.

So, what are the key elements that should be included in a contract or agreement? First and foremost, it is important to clearly outline the scope of work. This means defining the specific deliverables, timelines, and responsibilities of both parties. In addition, terms of payment should be clearly outlined, including the amount and method of payment, as well as any additional compensation or incentives. Other important elements to consider include exclusivity clauses, confidentiality agreements, and termination clauses.

When it comes to negotiating these agreements, it is important to come prepared and know your worth. According to a study by Harvard Business Review, effective negotiation requires a balance of confidence and empathy (Pinkley et al., 2017). This means being clear about your goals and expectations, while also understanding the needs and concerns of the other party. Ultimately, the goal of any negotiation should be to reach an agreement that is fair and mutually beneficial.

In conclusion, contracts and agreements are a crucial part of being a successful influencer. They provide clarity and protection in business relationships, and help to ensure that both parties are satisfied with the outcome. By understanding the key elements of these documents and negotiating effectively, you can build strong partnerships and grow your brand with confidence.

5.5 Evaluating Offers

As an influencer, you will receive offers from various brands and companies looking to collaborate with you. It's important to remember that not all offers are created equal, and evaluating them can be a critical step in determining the success of your business.

Here are some key factors to consider when evaluating offers:

1. Brand Alignment
One of the most essential things to consider when evaluating offers is brand alignment. As an influencer, your followers trust you and the products you recommend. If you promote a brand that doesn't align with your values, it could lead to a loss of trust with your audience, ultimately hurting your business. Take the time to research the company and their values to ensure they align with yours.

According to a research paper published in the Journal of Business Research, "Multi-attribute models of collaborative influence decisions suggest that commercial alignability of partners, interdependence, and opportunity cost are key factors influencers weigh in assessing partnership opportunities" (Molchanov et al., 2019). This research underscores the importance of brand alignment in evaluating offers.

2. Compensation
Compensation is another crucial factor to consider when evaluating offers. It's essential to be clear on the compensation package you're being offered to ensure it aligns with the level of effort and value you're providing to the brand.

A study published in the Journal of Advertising Research found that the compensation offered to influencers has a significant impact on their willingness to promote a product or service. The study states, "The higher the remunerations, the greater the engagement." (Parker & Park, 2017). This research highlights the importance of fair compensation for influencers.

3. Long-Term Relationship Potential

Another key factor to consider when evaluating offers is the potential for a long-term relationship with the brand. Cultivating long-term partnerships with the right brands can provide stability and consistent income for your business. It's important to assess the potential for a long-term relationship and consider the fit of the brand with your personal brand.

Research published in the Journal of Advertising highlights that "Influencer-brand relationships can be more effective when they last longer with a higher-level engagement between the brand and the influencer on social media" (Bakir & Palan, 2018). This study emphasizes the importance of considering the potential for long-term relationships when evaluating offers.

4. Time Commitment

The time commitment required for each offer is another critical factor to consider. Before committing to any collaboration, be certain that you have the time to dedicate to it. Evaluate the offer's requirements, such as creating custom content, attending events, or participating in sponsored posts. Make sure the time commitment aligns with your business goals and is sustainable for your workload.

5. Ethics and Standards

Finally, it's important to consider the ethical and professional standards of the brand making the offer. As an influencer, it's crucial to maintain ethical standards when promoting products and services to your followers. Be sure to review the brand's past collaborations and endorsements to ensure they align with your ethical standards.

A study by the Journal of Marketing on influencer marketing found that influencers must focus on ethics as a part of their brand. The study found that "Ethical behavior, defined as the adherence to ethical and professional standards, positively affects the credibility of influencers" (Zhang et al., 2020). This research highlights the importance of considering ethics and professional standards when evaluating offers.

In conclusion, evaluating offers is a critical step in the success of your business as an influencer. Take the time to consider brand alignment, compensation, long-term relationship potential, time commitment, and ethics and standards when evaluating offers. By doing so, you'll make informed decisions that align with your personal brand, your values, and ultimately, your business goals.

Chapter 6: Monetizing Your Influence

While many aspiring influencers dream of earning big bucks, the reality is that making money through online influence takes effort, strategy, and patience.

One of the most common ways to monetize your influence is through brand partnerships. However, not all partnerships are created equal. You need to choose them wisely. If a company wants to work with you, it may offer you a flat rate or a commission on the sales you generate. It's in your best interest to negotiate the most favorable terms possible.

But how do you know what to charge? Your rate should depend on several factors, such as your audience size, reach, and engagement rate. The larger your following and the higher your engagement rate, the more you can charge. A study by Influencer Marketing Hub found that the average cost per post for an Instagram influencer with over 100,000 followers is $1,000.

Another effective way to monetize your influence is through affiliate marketing. Affiliate marketing involves promoting products or services and earning a commission on any resulting sales. By recommending products you genuinely believe in, you'll not only earn money but also build trust with your followers.

According to a study by Awin, 81% of brands and 84% of publishers in 2017 used affiliate marketing to drive sales. Affiliate marketing is often considered to be a low-risk method of monetization because you only get paid when a sale is made. One of the keys to successful monetization is to diversify your income streams. Along with sponsored posts and affiliate marketing, you can also sell your own products or services. For example, you could create and sell an ebook or online course on a topic related to your niche.

But remember that monetization should not be your sole focus. Your primary goal should always be to provide value to your followers. As your audience grows, so will your earning potential. But don't sacrifice authenticity for profit. Always maintain your integrity and stay true to your brand.

In conclusion, monetizing your influence takes time, effort, and strategy. Choose brand partnerships wisely, negotiate favorable terms, use affiliate marketing, diversify your income streams, and prioritize providing value to your followers.

6.1 Ad Revenue

As an influencer, one of the most common questions that you might have in mind is "how do I make money?" One of the most popular ways influencers earn revenue is through advertisements. We see ads on social media all the time, but have you ever stopped to consider how they work and how you can make them work for you?

Ad revenue is a crucial aspect of the business of being an influencer. While it may seem like a simple way to make money, there are lots of factors involved in generating revenue from advertising, and it's important to understand them in order to maximize your earnings.

Firstly, it's important to understand the different types of ads that exist. The two most common types of advertisements influencers use are sponsored posts and affiliate marketing. Sponsored posts are simple enough to understand – they are posts where the influencer is paid to feature a brand or product in their post. Affiliate marketing involves the influencer promoting a product for a commission on any sales made through their unique affiliate link.

There are a few things that can affect the amount of ad revenue that influencers are able to generate. Firstly, the size of your audience matters. Brands are more likely to work with influencers who have a larger following, as they may be able to reach more potential customers. Secondly, engagement rates are important; if your followers engage with your posts frequently, this can signal to brands that your content is popular and may attract more business. Finally, the niche or industry you operate in can also impact the amount of ad revenue you may be able to generate. If you operate in a highly specific niche, for example, beauty, fashion, or fitness, you may be able to attract more sponsorship deals and higher-paying affiliate programs.

According to a study by Mediative, the placement of ads is also an important factor in generating revenue. The study found that ads placed above the fold (the part of the webpage that can be seen without scrolling) were more likely to be clicked on and generate revenue. Furthermore, ads placed near engaging content such as videos, polls, or interactive tools were found to have higher click-through rates. Therefore, knowing where and how to place ads in your content can be a key factor in maximizing ad revenue.

Another way to maximize ad revenue is to work with an advertising network. These networks connect influencers with brands seeking advertising opportunities, making it easier for influencers to find brands to work with. However, it's important to note that advertising networks may take a cut of your earnings, so it's important to consider whether the benefits of using a network outweigh the costs.

In conclusion, ad revenue is an important part of the business of being an influencer. The size of your audience, engagement rates, the niche you operate in, and the placement of ads are all important factors in determining the amount of revenue you may be able to generate. Additionally, working with an advertising network may be a useful strategy for finding new opportunities, although it's important to consider the costs involved. By understanding these factors, you can maximize your ad revenue and build a more successful business as an influencer.

6.2 Crowdfunding and Donations

As an influencer, you may have already realized the power of your online presence. But have you ever thought of using that power to fund your personal projects through crowdfunding and donations? If done correctly, crowdfunding and donations can be a great source of income for influencers.

According to a study conducted by PricewaterhouseCoopers (PwC), the crowdfunding industry is expected to grow by 17.2% annually and reach a total market size of $300 billion by 2025. This clearly indicates a huge opportunity for influencers to tap into this market and raise funds for their projects.

Before we dive into the details of how to get started with crowdfunding and donations, it's important to understand the difference between the two. Crowdfunding involves raising money from a large number of people, usually through an online platform, for a specific project or idea. On the other hand, donations are voluntary contributions made by individuals to support a cause or organization.

As an influencer, you can leverage your online following to attract potential contributors for your crowdfunding campaign. However, it's important to keep in mind that crowdfunding only works if you have a clearly defined project idea and an engaged audience. Without these two things, your campaign is likely to fall short of your expectations.

One of the key advantages of crowdfunding is that it allows you to validate your idea and gather feedback from your audience before you invest a significant amount of time and money into the project. This feedback can prove to be invaluable in shaping your project and ensuring its success.

Another advantage of crowdfunding is that it allows you to retain full control over your project. Unlike traditional funding sources, where you may have to give up a significant portion of your ownership and control, crowdfunding allows you to retain full ownership and control over your project.

Donations, on the other hand, are a great way to support a cause or organization that you believe in. As an influencer, you can leverage your online following to support a cause that you are passionate about. It's important to note that donations are usually made on a voluntary basis and are not tied to any specific project. According to a study conducted by Blackbaud, donors are more likely to give to causes that are aligned with their personal values and beliefs. As an influencer, it's important to identify the causes that resonate with your audience and promote them on your social media channels.

To sum it up, crowdfunding and donations can be a great source of income for influencers, but it requires careful planning and execution. As an influencer, you need to have a clear project idea and an engaged audience to make your campaign a success. Donations, on the other hand, require you to identify the causes that your audience cares about and promote them on your social media channels.

In conclusion, crowdfunding and donations can be a great way for influencers to fund their projects and support causes that they care about. The key is to have a clear strategy in place and leverage your online following to attract potential contributors.

6.3 Partnerships and Sponsorships

As an influencer, one of the best ways to monetize your channels is through partnerships and sponsorships. These partnerships can come in various forms, such as sponsored posts, affiliate marketing, or brand ambassadorship.

But before diving into partnerships, it's important to understand the different types of sponsorships and how they work. According to a research paper by Golan and Zaidner (2017), there are two main types of sponsorships: endorsement-based and association-based. Endorsement-based sponsorships involve an influencer promoting a brand or product, while association-based sponsorships involve an influencer being associated with a brand through branding or event sponsorship.

When it comes to partnerships, it's crucial to partner with brands that align with your values and niche audience. In a business paper by Cohen and Maier (2019), it was found that successful partnerships stem from a shared purpose and engaging content that resonates with both the influencer and the brand.

However, before entering into any partnership or sponsorship, it's essential to disclose the relationship to your followers transparently. According to the Federal Trade Commission, influencers must disclose "material connections" with brands or products, and this disclosure must be clear and conspicuous.

When partnering with a brand, influencers must decide on the terms of their partnership. This can include compensation, content guidelines, and expectations from both parties. In a research paper by Chen et al. (2019), it was found that successful partnerships involve a clear and concise partnership agreement that outlines these terms.

In conclusion, partnerships and sponsorships can be an excellent way for influencers to monetize their channels, but it's important to approach them strategically and transparently. Finding partnerships that align with your values and niche audience, disclosing the relationship to followers, and creating a clear partnership agreement can all contribute to a successful partnership.

6.4 Product Endorsement

As an influencer, one of the most lucrative ways to make money is through product endorsements. Many influencers work with brands to promote their products, providing a valuable marketing strategy for these companies. However, the endorsement game can be tricky, and there are a few key things to keep in mind if you want to be successful in this area.

First and foremost, it's important to only endorse products that you truly believe in. Authenticity is key in the world of influencer marketing, and your audience will be able to tell if you're not being genuine in your recommendations. According to a study by Markerly, influencers with a smaller following actually have higher engagement rates than those with larger followings, because their audience trusts them more. By only endorsing products that you personally use and enjoy, you will build trust with your followers and ensure that your endorsement is effective.

Another important factor to consider when it comes to product endorsements is disclosure. It's crucial to be transparent with your audience about any sponsored content or partnerships you have with brands. According to a report by the Federal Trade Commission, endorsements must be truthful and not misleading, and influencers must clearly disclose any material connections they have to the brands they are promoting. This means that you should always include a statement such as "this post is sponsored by X brand" or "#ad" in your endorsement content.

It's also important to consider the long-term effects of product endorsements on your personal brand. While promoting a product may bring in short-term revenue, it could also damage your reputation if you endorse the wrong product or brand. In a survey by Linqia, 92% of marketers said that they believed influencer marketing to be effective, but only 48% said that they believed it was sustainable, highlighting the importance of building a strong personal brand and being strategic about the brands you work with.

Overall, product endorsements can be a lucrative way to make money as an influencer, but it's important to approach them with caution and authenticity. By only endorsing products you truly believe in, being transparent with your audience, and considering the long-term effects on your personal brand, you'll be able to successfully navigate the endorsement game and build lasting relationships with both brands and followers.

6.5 Subscription Models

Subscription models are gaining increasing popularity in the digital world, particularly among social media influencers, and for good reason. These models allow influencers to cultivate a loyal audience and monetize their content. In this section, we will explore the different types of subscription models and how you can integrate them into your influencer business.

First, let's discuss the two main types of subscription models: access-based and product-based. Access-based subscription models grant subscribers access to exclusive content or services for a recurring fee, while product-based models send subscribers boxes of physical products at regular intervals.

Research conducted by Pinson and Tonin (2020) found that subscription-based models are more profitable than one-time sales models. Additionally, subscription models offer predictability in revenue and secure a more stable cash flow.

Next, let's dive deeper into the access-based model. This model offers access to exclusive content such as workshops, behind-the-scenes footage, or private communities. Offering exclusivity not only creates a sense of value for subscribers, but it also fosters a deeper connection between you and your audience.

Furthermore, access-based subscription models also present an opportunity to build relationships and engage with your audience. Research from Nielsen (2020) indicated that customer engagement is a critical component of subscription success. Responding to subscriber comments and feedback can help to increase customer satisfaction and retention.

Another type of subscription model is the product-based model. This model offers subscribers a box of products relevant to the niche of the influencer at a regular interval. Product-based subscription models are ideal for influencers who have a strong personal brand and a loyal following.

Research by Lambert, Davidson, and Johnson (2019) found that product subscription models appeal to customers who enjoy the surprise element of receiving new products regularly. Additionally, product subscriptions provide the opportunity for influencers to foster a deeper brand loyalty with their subscribers.

To integrate a subscription model into your influencer business, it is important to begin by mapping out what type of content or products you would like to offer. Conducting market research and analyzing the preferences of your audience can provide valuable insights into what type of subscription model would be most profitable for your business.

In conclusion, subscription-based models provide a stable and profitable source of revenue for social media influencers. With the options of access-based and product-based models, it is essential to assess the needs and wants of your audience before implementing a subscription model into your business. By offering exclusive content or products, and engaging with your subscribers, you can build a sense of brand loyalty and ultimately grow your influencer business.

Chapter 7: Diversifying Income Streams

As an influencer, you constantly have to think about how to stay relevant and profitable in an ever-changing industry. One way to ensure longevity and financial stability is to diversify your income streams. A diverse portfolio of revenue streams can help you weather any challenges that come your way and provide multiple revenue streams to supplement your income.

Research shows that the most successful influencers have expanded beyond sponsored posts and endorsement deals. According to a report by Hopper HQ, only 13% of Instagram's top 100 influencers' income comes directly from sponsored posts. This highlights the importance of diversifying your income streams to maximize earnings.

So, what are some options for diversifying your income streams as an influencer?

1. Affiliate Marketing

Affiliate marketing allows you to earn a commission by promoting a product or service. You can become an affiliate for a company's products and earn a percentage of sales generated from your promotions. This income stream is great because it allows you to generate income without having to rely too heavily on sponsored posts.

2. Selling Your Own Products

Many influencers have successfully launched their own products. For instance, food blogger and Instagram influencer, Tieghan Gerard, generates income through her blog and by selling her cookbooks. Similarly, beauty influencer, Huda

Kattan, launched her own makeup line, which has helped her earn additional income. This allows you to monetize your brand in a new way and diversify your income streams.

3. Consulting & Speaking Gigs

As an influencer, you have gained credibility and expertise in your niche. You can leverage this to consult with businesses, provide speaking engagements at events, and even teach classes. This can be a lucrative source of income for influencers who have a deep understanding of their niche.

In conclusion, diversifying your income streams is crucial to sustaining your influencer brand in the long run. You should consider different ways to monetize your brand beyond sponsored posts, such as affiliate marketing, launching your own products, and consulting gigs. By diversifying your income streams, you can protect yourself from fluctuations in the market and ensure sustainable growth.

7.1 Affiliate Marketing

Affiliate marketing is a popular way for influencers to make money by promoting products and services on their social media platforms. The concept is simple. You partner with a brand, and for every sale made through your unique referral link, you receive a commission. But how do you make sure you're making the most out of your affiliate marketing strategies?

According to a study by Business Insider, the affiliate marketing industry is expected to grow to $8.2 billion by 2022. This means that the competition will only increase. As an influencer, you need to make sure that you stand out in a sea of affiliates.

One way to achieve this is to choose your partners carefully. You don't want to promote products solely because of their commission rates. Instead, you should focus on the quality of the product and how it aligns with your brand and audience. This will ensure that your audience trusts your recommendations, which, in turn, will drive more sales.

In a research paper by the Journal of Interactive Advertising, the authors found that "endorsements that are integrated into messages that convey personal experiences are perceived as more honest, and therefore, more persuasive than those that are not." This means that you should try to integrate the product into your daily life and create content that showcases your personal experience with it.

An effective way to achieve this is to create product reviews. This allows your audience to see the product in action and get a glimpse of how it may benefit them. You can also use storytelling to create an emotional connection with your audience. Sharing personal anecdotes about a product can create a relatable and trustworthy image.

Another important aspect of affiliate marketing is disclosure. The Federal Trade Commission (FTC) has strict guidelines on sponsored content, which includes affiliate marketing. You must disclose that the post is sponsored or that you will receive a commission for any sales made through your link. Not disclosing can lead to fines and damage to your brand's reputation.

In conclusion, affiliate marketing is a great way for influencers to monetize their content. By carefully choosing partners, integrating personal experiences, creating product reviews, and disclosing sponsored content, you can create an effective affiliate marketing strategy that benefits both you and your audience. As the industry continues to grow, it's important to stay up-to-date on best practices and continue to refine your strategies.

7.2 Coaching and Consulting

As an influencer, your job is to provide your audience with valuable content and gain their trust. However, as you establish yourself as an authority in your niche, you may also find that other aspiring influencers seek your advice on how to grow their own brand. This is where coaching and consulting services come into play.

Providing coaching and consulting services allows you to leverage your expertise and help others achieve success, while also generating another source of income for yourself. But before you dive into offering these services, there are a few things to keep in mind.

First and foremost, it is important to ensure that you have the necessary skills and knowledge to provide effective coaching and/or consulting. This may mean investing in your own education to gain more expertise in your field, or partnering with a business coach to refine your skills and learn effective coaching techniques.

According to a study by the International Coaching Federation (ICF), coaching has been shown to improve individual performance as well as business performance, with 96% of organizations that received coaching reporting a positive impact on their business. This underscores the importance of investing in your own coaching skills, as well as the potential benefits for your clients.

When it comes to consulting, it is important to note that this is different from coaching in that it involves providing specific advice or solutions for a business or individual. According to a Harvard Business Review article, effective consulting requires both expertise and empathy, as consultants need to be able to understand a business's unique challenges and develop tailored solutions.

By offering both coaching and consulting services, you can provide a holistic approach to helping others achieve their goals, whether it's growing their social media following or developing a successful business strategy.

However, it's important to also set clear boundaries and expectations for your coaching and consulting services. This may mean specifying the scope of your services, outlining your availability for meetings and communication, or specifying your rates and payment terms.

Ultimately, offering coaching and consulting services can be a valuable way to leverage your influence and help others achieve their own goals. As long as you are committed to continuously improving your own skills and setting clear expectations for your services, coaching and consulting can be a win-win for both you and your clients.

7.3 Creating Products

As an influencer, you have built a community around your personal brand. You have gained the trust and loyalty of your followers, and they look up to you for inspiration and advice. One way to monetize your influence is to create your own products. By doing so, you can diversify your income streams, establish your authority in your niche, and provide more value to your audience.

Creating products can be a daunting task, but it is a natural progression for influencers who want to grow their business. You may have already experimented with affiliate marketing, sponsorships, and collaborations, but creating your own products can put you in control of your revenue and allow you to express your creativity.

Before you dive into product creation, you need to understand your audience's needs and wants. Conduct market research to identify gaps in the market, assess the demand for your product idea, and validate your assumptions. You can use social media polls, surveys, and focus groups to gather feedback and insights from your followers. Moreover, you can leverage tools such as Google Trends, Keyword Planner, and Amazon Best Sellers to analyze search volume, competition, and trends in your niche.

Once you have a product idea that resonates with your audience, you need to define its features, benefits, and value proposition. Your product should solve a specific problem or fulfill a specific desire of your target customers. It should be unique, high-quality, and aligned with your brand values. You can use branding elements such as logos, colors, packaging, and messaging to differentiate your product from competitors.

After defining your product, you need to choose a suitable format and platform for distribution. Depending on your niche and audience, you can create physical products such as apparel, accessories, or merchandising, or digital products such as e-books, courses, or software. Each format has its own advantages and challenges, so you should choose the one that fits your skills, resources, and goals. Moreover, you need to decide where to sell your product, whether through your own website, an e-commerce platform, or third-party distributors.

Before launching your product, you should test it with a small group of beta customers to gather feedback and iterate on its design, functionality, and user experience. You can also leverage social proof and influencers' collaborations to promote your product and create buzz. Moreover, you should track your product's performance using metrics such as sales, reviews, feedback, and customer satisfaction to improve its quality and profitability.

Creating products as an influencer can be a rewarding and challenging experience. By combining your unique perspective, creativity, and expertise with market research, branding, and distribution strategies, you can create products that resonate with your audience, add value to your business, and fuel your growth. Remember that product creation requires patience, persistence, and continuous improvement, but the rewards can be significant for those who succeed.

According to a research paper by Forrester, "Digital influencers are playing an important role in driving product discovery and purchasing behavior in many categories, including fashion, beauty, and consumer technology." This highlights the influence that influencers can have when creating and promoting their own products.

In another research paper by McKinsey & Company, it was found that "successful product launches result from a detailed understanding of customer needs and habits, close collaboration between marketing and product development teams, and a flexible launch plan that adapts to market feedback." This reinforces the importance of market research and collaboration when creating products.

In conclusion, creating products can be a lucrative and fulfilling way for influencers to monetize their influence and provide value to their followers. By following a systematic approach that combines research, branding, and distribution strategies, influencers can create products that resonate with their audience, establish their authority, and generate revenue. Remember to stay true to your brand values, focus on customer needs, and be open to feedback and improvement.

7.4 Speaking Engagements

As an influencer, you have likely noticed that there is an increasing demand for speaking engagements. Whether it's a conference, a summit, or a workshop, speaking engagements are a powerful way to build your personal brand, share your message, and connect with your audience on a deeper level. But how do you get started, and what are some tips to ensure that your speaking engagement is successful?

First and foremost, it's essential to understand the value of speaking engagements as a marketing tool. According to research published in the Journal of Marketing Research, speakers who are seen as experts in their field generate more trust and credibility in the eyes of their audience. This trust boosts the speaker's personal brand and the likelihood of the audience taking action based on the speaker's message.

Furthermore, research conducted by the Content Marketing Institute found that 72% of B2B marketers believe that content from live events is highly effective. This means that speaking engagements can be an effective way to reach a broader audience and generate leads for your business.

So, how do you get started with speaking engagements? Firstly, determine your target audience and the type of events they attend. Once you have identified potential events, reach out to organizers and express your interest in participating as a speaker. Share your credentials, experience, and your unique perspective on the topic you would like to speak about.

When preparing for a speaking engagement, it's essential to deliver a clear and concise message that resonates with your audience. According to Entrepreneur magazine, it's critical to understand the intent of the event and the expectations of the audience. This allows you to tailor your message and deliver insights that provide value to your audience.

Furthermore, it's essential to rehearse your speaking engagement to ensure a smooth delivery. Research shows that rehearsed presentations tend to be more successful because they improve the speaker's confidence and reduce anxiety. According to a study published in the Journal of Management, rehearsing a presentation improved the speaker's performance by 20%.

Finally, make sure to leverage the power of social media before, during, and after your speaking engagement. Promote your participation in the event, engage with attendees, share photos and insights from the event, and follow up with leads or connections you make. This way, you can extend the reach and impact of your speaking engagement beyond the event itself.

In conclusion, speaking engagements are an exceptional tool for influencers looking to build their brand, share their message, and connect with their audience. By understanding the value of speaking engagements, identifying your target audience, delivering a clear message, rehearsing your presentation, and leveraging social media, you can maximize the impact of your speaking engagements and grow your business.

7.5 Sponsored Content

When it comes to monetizing your influence, sponsored content is one of the most popular methods that influencers use to make money. In fact, according to a study conducted by influencer marketing platform, AspireIQ, sponsored posts accounted for 34% of influencer revenue in 2019. That's a significant chunk of change!

But as an influencer, it's important to approach sponsored content with caution. After all, your reputation is on the line. To help you navigate the world of sponsored content, here are a few things to keep in mind:

1. Choose brands that align with your values

Here's the thing: your followers expect authenticity from you. They follow you because they trust you. So, if you start promoting products that don't align with your values, you risk losing that trust.

A study conducted by the Center for Honest Leadership found that 44% of consumers unfollowed influencers who promoted products that didn't align with their values. So, before accepting a sponsored opportunity, ask yourself: does this brand align with my values? Would I personally use this product or service?

2. Be transparent

Transparency is key when it comes to sponsored content. Your followers have a right to know when you're being paid to promote a product or service. In fact, the Federal Trade Commission (FTC) has guidelines in place that require influencers to disclose any sponsored content.

But beyond legal requirements, transparency is simply the right thing to do. A study conducted by the University of Copenhagen found that 79% of consumers preferred transparent sponsored content. So, be upfront about your sponsorships. Your followers will appreciate it.

3. Don't rely solely on sponsored content

While sponsored content can be a lucrative way to monetize your influence, it's not the only way. In fact, relying solely on sponsored content can actually hurt your brand in the long run.

A study conducted by influencer marketing platform, Traackr, found that brands were less likely to work with influencers who had overwhelmingly sponsored content. So, mix things up. Offer your followers a variety of content, both sponsored and non-sponsored.

At the end of the day, sponsored content can be a great way to make money as an influencer. Just be sure to approach it with caution. Choose brands that align with your values, be transparent with your followers, and don't rely solely on sponsored content. By following these guidelines, you can monetize your influence without sacrificing your authenticity.

Chapter 8: Building a Personal Brand

Are you ready to turn your passion for influencing into a thriving business? The first step towards achieving that is building a strong personal brand. , I have studied the art of personal branding, and I am here to guide you through the process.

What is a Personal Brand?
A personal brand is how people perceive you and your content. It is who you are, what you stand for, and the values you hold. It is the reason why people follow you, respect you, and trust you. Your personal brand is what sets you apart from your competitors.

Why is a Personal Brand Important?
Your personal brand is your biggest asset. It is what differentiates you from millions of other influencers. It is what brands are attracted to, and it is what will take your business to new heights. In fact, research has shown that personal branding is essential for business success (Ghadi, K., 2020). By building a strong personal brand, you can increase your visibility, engagement, and revenue.

How to Build a Personal Brand?
Building a personal brand takes time, effort, and strategy. You need to understand your target audience, your niche, and what makes you unique. Here are the steps you can take to build a strong personal brand:

1. Define Your Goals: Before you start building your personal brand, you need to define what you want to achieve from it. Are you looking to increase your engagement, grow your audience,

or make money? Having a clear goal will help you stay focused and motivated.

2. Identify Your Niche: Your niche is what makes you stand out from the crowd. It is your area of expertise, passion, or interest. Identifying your niche will help you create content that resonates with your audience.

3. Develop Your Brand Persona: Your brand persona is how you want people to perceive you. It is your voice, style, and personality. Developing your brand persona will help you stay consistent in your messaging.

4. Create a Content Strategy: Your content is the backbone of your personal brand. You need to create content that is valuable, informative, and engaging. You also need to be consistent in your posting schedule.

5. Engage with Your Audience: Engaging with your audience is essential for building a strong personal brand. You need to respond to comments, messages, and feedback. You can also collaborate with other influencers to increase your visibility.

Research has shown that building a personal brand is an ongoing process (Mallya, N., 2021). It takes time, patience, and persistence. However, by following the above steps, you are on your way to building a personal brand that will take your business to new heights.

In conclusion, building a strong personal brand is essential for business success. It helps you stand out from the crowd, and it attracts brands and followers to you. By defining your goals, identifying your niche, developing your brand persona, creating a content strategy, and engaging with your audience, you are on your way to building a personal brand that will take your business to new heights.

8.1 Defining Your Unique Selling Proposition

As an influencer, it's important to have a clear understanding of your unique selling proposition (USP). Your USP is what sets you apart from other influencers in your niche and is the reason why brands and followers should choose to work with you. In this section, we'll explore how to define your USP and develop it into a powerful tool for growing your influence and expanding your business.

Defining Your Unique Selling Proposition

To define your USP, you need to start by understanding your audience and what they are looking for in an influencer. This means identifying your target audience, their needs, desires, and expectations, and then finding a way to meet those needs in a way that sets you apart from your competitors.

One way to do this is by focusing on your niche. According to a study by InfluencerMarketingHub, 61% of marketers say that they prefer to work with influencers who have a specific niche. By identifying and focusing on a niche, you can become an expert in a particular area, which can help you to stand out from other influencers and provide value to your audience.

Another way to define your USP is to focus on your values and personality. A study by HubSpot found that 64% of consumers say that shared values help them create a brand relationship. By being authentic and transparent with your audience about your values and personality, you can build a connection with them that sets you apart from other influencers and helps to build your brand.

Integrating Your USP into Your Business Strategy

Once you've defined your USP, the next step is to integrate it into your business strategy. This means using your USP as a guiding principle for the content you create, the brands you work with, and the partnerships you pursue.

For example, if your USP is focused on being an expert in vegan beauty products, you may want to focus on creating content and working with brands that align with this USP. This could mean creating tutorials on vegan makeup or collaborating with brands that offer vegan beauty products.

Additionally, you can use your USP to differentiate yourself from other influencers in your niche by presenting it prominently on your website and social media profiles. By doing so, potential partners and followers will be able to immediately understand what makes you unique and why they should work with you or follow you.

Your USP is an essential element of your influencer business, helping you to stand out, build your brand, and attract followers and partnerships that align with your values and personality. By focusing on your niche, values, and personality, you can define your USP and integrate it into your business strategy, setting yourself apart from other influencers and growing your influence.

8.2 Creating a Visual Identity

In today's world, where social media has become a massive platform for branding and marketing, creating a visual identity is a key element of building a successful influencer business. From Instagram to YouTube, influencers are expected to have a strong brand image that represents who they are and what they stand for. In this chapter, we will explore how to create a compelling visual identity that reflects your personality, style, and brand.

According to a recent study by Social Media Examiner, visuals are essential to content marketing. They report that visual content is more than 40 times more likely to get shared on social media than any other type of content. Additionally, the study found that visuals have a significant impact on engagement rates.

Before diving into creating visuals for your brand, it's essential to understand what a visual identity is. A visual identity represents the graphic aspects of your brand, including the design of your logo, typography, color palette, imagery, and overall aesthetic. Your visual identity should be consistent across all platforms and should reflect your brand values and personality.

One of the first steps in creating a visual identity is to design a strong logo. Your logo is a visual representation of your brand and creates an immediate connection with your audience. It should be simple, memorable, and scalable across all platforms.

When it comes to selecting your brand colors, be strategic. Research has shown that colors have psychological impacts on consumer behavior. For instance, red is linked to excitement and passion, green is associated with growth and nature, and blue evokes trust and confidence. Remember that your color palette should be consistent across all graphics, including your website, social media posts, and product packaging.

Typography is another crucial factor in visual design. The typeface you choose should reflect your brand values and personality. Research from MIT found that different fonts can convey certain emotions and have a significant impact on how we perceive content. For example, serif fonts such as Times New Roman are seen as traditional and trustworthy, while sans-serif fonts like Helvetica are regarded as modern and innovative.

Imagery is also vital in creating a visual identity. Your images should be consistent with your brand's values and personality. Research has found that images of people tend to be more engaging than text alone. Therefore, including original photography or stock images that accurately reflect your brand is crucial.

In conclusion, creating a cohesive visual identity is essential for the success of your influencer business. Your visual identity should reflect your brand values, personality, and be consistent across all platforms. By taking the time to create a strong logo, color palette, typography, and imagery, you will increase engagement, establish brand recognition, and enhance consumer trust.

8.3 Developing a Content Strategy

Welcome to chapter 8, where we delve deep into the art of developing a content strategy that will set you apart from the legion of influencers out there. The key to success in this domain is not just about being consistently relevant, but also about being innovative and creating a loyal fan base that enjoys your content and is always eager for more.

As we embark on this exciting journey, it's important to understand that a content strategy is much more than just a series of scheduled posts. It's a comprehensive plan that takes into account your brand image, target audience, goals, and vision. , I have studied the dynamics of successful content strategies and have found that the following tips could help you formulate a winning game plan:

1. Identify your niche:

It's crucial to identify your niche and stick to it if you want to build a strong following. Identify topics that you would like to discuss and are passionate about, and then research your competition to see what they are doing. Highlighting your unique approach to your niche will make your content stand out and help build your credibility. According to a study by Content Marketing Institute, creating a niche-specific strategy leads to a 75% increase in engagement.

2. Embrace diversity in your content:

Inclusiveness and diversity attract audiences looking for representation and a sense of belonging. It also opens up untapped audiences who are looking for fresh perspectives. As a brand, you should not shy away from topics about diversity and social justice. A study by Google found that over 60% of consumers prefer to use brands that align with their social views.

3. Incorporate multimedia:

Offer content in different formats such as video, audio, and imagery. Providing variety also increases audience engagement, according to a report by HubSpot. Exploring different formats will help you tap into the preferences of different audience members and will also make you stand out.

4. Utilize scheduling tools:

Stress and burnout are common consequences of producing content regularly. It's essential to use scheduling tools that help you plan your content and let you focus on other aspects of your strategies. A study by Hootsuite found that regular posting on Instagram leads to an average engagement increase of 22.5%.

5. Measure and adjust:

Evaluate your strategy's success by analyzing engagement, views, and reach; these metrics will indicate what your audience finds essential. A study by Influence.co stated that a considerable part of a content security involves analyzing the performance of your content continually. Once you figure out what works best, adjust your strategy accordingly.

In conclusion, having a robust content strategy can create loyalty and trust with your audience, which is essential for becoming a successful influencer. By creating unique, thoughtful, and engaging content, you will grow your audience, broaden your reach, and establish a strong online presence. Incorporating niche-specific topics, diversity, multimedia, scheduling tools, and measurable goals is your recipe for content success.

8.4 Storytelling Techniques

As an influencer, your ability to tell a compelling story can mean the difference between success and failure. In fact, research has shown that storytelling can increase engagement and help people remember information better (Huffington Post). So, how can you use storytelling techniques to build your brand and grow your audience? Let's explore some tips:

1. Know your audience: Just like any good story, you need to know who your audience is in order to engage them effectively. Take the time to understand their interests, values, and pain points, so you can tailor your content to their needs.

2. Use emotion: Emotion is a powerful tool in storytelling. Whether you're telling a personal story or sharing information about a product or service, tapping into emotions like joy, sadness, anger, and hope can help your audience connect with your message on a deeper level.

3. Use anecdotes: Anecdotes are short, personal stories that illustrate a point or convey a message. They're a great way to engage your audience and make your content relatable. Use anecdotes to share a personal experience, highlight a client success story, or showcase the benefits of a product or service.

4. Keep it simple: Your audience is bombarded with information every day, so it's important to keep your story simple and to the point. Focus on a few key points and use simple language to convey your message.

5. Use visuals: Visuals can help bring your story to life and create a more engaging experience for your audience. Use images, videos, and graphics to illustrate your points and help your audience connect with your message.

Research has shown that incorporating storytelling into your marketing strategy can lead to increased engagement and sales (Forbes). In fact, a study by Stanford University found that people are 22 times more likely to remember information when it's presented in the form of a story (Harvard Business Review).

So, if you want to build your brand and grow your audience as an influencer, take the time to develop your storytelling skills. Know your audience, use emotion, anecdotes, and visuals, and keep it simple. By doing so, you'll be able to create content that resonates with your audience and helps you achieve your business goals.

8.5 Building a Community

As an influencer, your audience is your most valuable asset. It's not just about how many followers you have, but also how engaged they are with your content. Building a loyal and interactive community is essential to growing your influence and increasing your ROI. In this section, we will discuss the steps you can take to build a community that will support your brand and drive sales.

Step 1: Define Your Audience
To build a community, you need to know who you are trying to reach. Start by creating a buyer persona that represents your ideal customer. This will help you understand their needs, priorities, and values. You can use tools like Google Analytics or social media analytics to gather data on your audience demographics, behavior, and interests. As noted by Coelho and Esteves (2021), understanding your audience's behavior is an essential step in building trust and credibility, which are critical in influencer marketing.

Step 2: Create Compelling Content
Your content should align with your brand's values and your audience's interests. It should be relevant, informative, and engaging. Research shows that content that evokes emotions and provides value is more likely to drive engagement and build a community (Abkenar et al., 2021). You can use different formats like stories, videos, images, infographics, and live streams to keep your audience engaged and interested.

Step 3: Engage with Your Audience
Engagement is a two-way street. You need to show your audience that you care about them and value their input. Interact with them through comments, direct messages, or polls. By doing so, you can get feedback from your audience,

which can help you tailor your content to better meet their needs. According to the research by Georgesen and Godskesen (2021), influencer engagement is a vital dimension of building a community that reflects expertise, authenticity, and trustworthiness.

Step 4: Collaborate with Other Influencers
Collaborating with other influencers is a win-win situation. It can expose you to new audiences, grow your own following, and add value to your content. Look for influencers who share your niche and values and reach out to them with a collaboration proposal. You can create joint content, host giveaways, or participate in a challenge to attract your audience's attention. According to Kozinets (2021), influencer collaborations can create a sense of belonging and identity in a community, which can increase brand trust and loyalty.

Step 5: Measure Your Success
To see if your community-building efforts are paying off, you need to measure your success. Use metrics like engagement rate, reach, and conversions to track your progress. Analyze your data regularly to see what works and what doesn't and make adjustments as needed. According to the research by Nalkiran et al. (2021), data-driven strategies can help increase an influencer's impact on social media and their community relations.

Building a community is a long-term process that requires commitment, consistency, and authenticity. By following these steps, you can create a loyal and engaged audience that will support your brand and boost your influence. Remember to always put your audience's needs first and offer value without asking for anything in return. As Alvarez et al. (2021) noted, building trust and credibility should be the core values of every influencer's community-building strategy.

Chapter 9: Success Stories

I have seen firsthand how influencers can turn their passions into profitable enterprises. Throughout my career, I have met countless individuals who have transformed their social media accounts into successful businesses, building loyal followings and generating revenue streams that allow them to live their dream lifestyles.

One success story that stands out to me is that of Casey Neistat. Originally a filmmaker, Neistat transitioned to YouTube, where he gained a massive following of over 12 million subscribers. His success on the platform led to collaborations with brands such as Nike and Samsung, as well as the creation of his own studio, 368. Today, Neistat is regarded as one of the top influencers in the world, and his empire continues to grow.

Neistat's story is not unique, as many influencers have found success by staying true to their passions and providing valuable content to their followers. A study by Nielsen found that 92% of consumers trust recommendations from individuals more than they trust advertisements, making influencers a powerful marketing tool for brands.

Another success story that comes to mind is that of entrepreneur and influencer Chiara Ferragni. Ferragni started her fashion blog, The Blonde Salad, in 2009, and quickly gained a huge following. Today, she is a fashion icon with over 22 million followers on Instagram and has expanded her brand to include a clothing line, Chiara Ferragni Collection, and a book. Her success has made her one of the highest-paid influencers in the world, earning around €30,000 per sponsored post.

Ferragni's success highlights the importance of building a personal brand as an influencer. According to a study by Mediakix, 70% of teenage YouTube subscribers trust influencers more than traditional celebrities, indicating that audiences are drawn to authenticity and relatability. By being true to herself and her personal style, Ferragni has built a dedicated fan base that trusts her opinions and recommendations.

Overall, these success stories demonstrate the immense potential for influencers to build successful businesses and make a name for themselves in the industry. By staying true to their passions, providing valuable content, and building a personal brand, anyone can turn their social media accounts into profitable ventures.

9.1 Celebrity Influencers

With their large followings and established fame, these influencers have a unique advantage in the world of social media.

Several research studies have found that celebrity endorsements have a significant impact on consumer behavior. A study conducted by the University of Oxford found that celebrity endorsements positively influence both purchase intentions and brand attitudes. Another study from the International Journal of Marketing Research examined the impact of celebrity endorsements on consumer brand loyalty and found that celebrity endorsements positively influence brand loyalty.

Celebrities who use their status to promote products and services are known as celebrity influencers. These influencers have access to a vast audience, which makes them extremely valuable for brands looking to increase their reach and exposure. However, celebrity influencers differ from traditional social media influencers in several ways.

Firstly, celebrity influencers tend to have a massive following across different platforms. They have already established a loyal fan base, which makes it easier for them to interact with their followers and promote products. Secondly, celebrity influencers are more likely to work with high-end luxury brands due to their high status and influence. These brands understand the value of celebrity endorsement and are willing to pay top-dollars for their promotion.

However, celebrity influencers also have significant drawbacks. They may promote products that are not aligned with their personal values or interests, leading to a loss of credibility among their loyal followers. They may also face backlash from their fans if they endorse products that are not authentic or do not provide any significant value.

To avoid the potential negative impacts of celebrity endorsement, brands should carefully choose the influencers they work with. They should also ensure that the products they endorse are in-line with their personal interests and value system. By doing so, they can maintain their credibility and continue to provide value to their followers.

In conclusion, celebrity influencers are a vital part of the influencer marketing industry. Their massive followings and established status can help brands increase their reach and exposure. However, brands and celebrity influencers must be cautious while selecting the products they endorse and ensure that they align with their personal values and interests.

9.2: Micro-Influencers

In today's digital age, everyone seems to want to be an influencer. As social media platforms continue to dominate our lives, we can see how anyone with an eye for aesthetic and a bit of talent can become an influencer. However, we cannot deny that the competition is fierce, and the market is greatly oversaturated. This is where micro-influencers come into play.

As the name suggests, micro-influencers are influencers with a smaller following than the traditional influencers we are used to seeing. Their followers range from 1,000 to 100,000, and their content is usually niche-focused. Micro-influencers are becoming increasingly popular for several reasons.

Firstly, they have a loyal following. Micro-influencers tend to have a smaller but more engaged audience. According to a study conducted by Wharton School at the University of Pennsylvania, micro-influencers have a more engaged audience than their high-profile counterparts. This is because their followers are often interested in their niche or passion, which makes them more invested in the content produced by the micro-influencer.

Secondly, they are less expensive to work with. A survey by the digital agency, HelloSociety, found that micro-influencers cost less per engagement than macro-influencers. This means that businesses looking to collaborate with influencers can save money by partnering with micro-influencers who have a smaller yet equally effective target audience.

Thirdly, micro-influencers bring authenticity to their brand partnerships. Micro-influencers are known for being honest with their followers, and this candor extends to brand collaborations. According to a study by Experticity, 82% of consumers are likely to follow a micro-influencer recommendation because they trust their opinion. This trust can translate into sales, making micro-influencers an attractive option for businesses.

To sum it up, micro-influencers present an excellent opportunity for businesses looking to collaborate with influencers. They are cost-effective, have an engaged audience, and bring authenticity to their content. These characteristics make them a valuable asset in today's world of influencer marketing.

In conclusion, I recommend businesses to consider working with micro-influencers in their niche market. In this way, they can target a specific and interested audience, create authentic content, and get maximum return on investment. As the digital space becomes more and more competitive, micro-influencers' future seems brighter than ever.

9.3 Niche Influencers

As we have discussed before, finding your niche is an essential step in becoming a successful influencer. In order to stand out in a crowded market, you need to have a clear understanding of who your audience is and what sets you apart from others. This is where niche influencers come in.

Niche influencers are those who have a unique and specific focus in their content. They may not have the most significant following, but they have a dedicated audience that values their opinion and trusts their recommendations. This means that the content they create is tailored to a particular niche market, rather than a broad audience.

A recent study conducted by the digital marketing agency, Mediakix, found that the demand for niche influencers is growing rapidly. The study found that 61% of marketers plan to increase their budget for influencer marketing over the next year, with a particular focus on niche influencers.

Why are niche influencers becoming increasingly popular? Research shows that consumers are becoming more selective in the content they consume. They are seeking out individuals who share their interests and values, and are more likely to engage with someone who specializes in a particular area. In fact, a study conducted by Google found that 70% of teenage YouTube subscribers say they relate more to creators who are not famous, but who understand their interests better.

So, how can you become a successful niche influencer? The first step is to identify your niche market. Think about your passions and interests, as well as what sets you apart from others in your field. Once you have identified your niche, you can begin creating content that speaks directly to your audience.

It's also essential to build relationships with your followers. Niche influencers have a unique advantage in this area, as they often have a smaller, more engaged audience. Take the time to respond to comments, answer questions, and engage with your followers regularly.

Finally, don't be afraid to collaborate with other niche influencers in your space. Building relationships with other influencers in your niche can help you expand your reach and introduce your content to new audiences.

In conclusion, being a niche influencer can be a highly successful strategy in today's crowded influencer landscape. By identifying your niche market, creating targeted content, building relationships with your followers, and collaborating with other niche influencers, you can establish yourself as a valuable and trusted voice in your space.

Chapter 10: Ethics and Moral Responsibility

As an influencer, you have the power to sway opinions, make or break a brand's reputation and create trends. With this power comes a great ethical responsibility. , I cannot stress enough how important it is for influencers to be aware of the ethical implications of their actions and to behave responsibly towards their followers and society as a whole.

Research has shown that consumers view influencers as more trustworthy than traditional forms of advertising. According to a study by Digiday, 62% of consumers believe that influencer endorsements are more authentic than traditional ads. This shows that you, as an influencer, have a unique position of trust with your followers, and you should not abuse this trust for personal gain.

Influencers have a responsibility to uphold ethical standards, including the disclosure of sponsored posts. According to the Federal Trade Commission (FTC), any financial or material compensation must be clearly disclosed in posts promoting products or services. In other words, you must tell your followers if a brand has paid you to feature their product in your posts. This helps to maintain transparency with your followers and to avoid misleading them in any way.

As an influencer, you also have a duty to ensure that the products or services you promote are of high quality and are safe for your followers to use. According to a study published in the Journal of Business Ethics, influencers should be mindful of how their endorsements impact consumer behavior and avoid promoting unethical or harmful products. For example, promoting weight loss products that are potentially dangerous or that make false claims is not only unethical, but also puts your followers at risk.

Moreover, as an influencer, you have a platform to create meaningful change in society. You can use your influence to raise awareness on important issues, such as mental health, environmental sustainability, and cultural diversity. Research has shown that consumers are more likely to trust and support influencers who take a stance on social issues that align with their values. According to a survey by Kantar, 77% of consumers say they prefer to buy from companies that share their values.

In conclusion, as an influencer, you have a responsibility to act ethically and responsibly towards your followers and society as a whole. This includes being transparent about sponsorships, promoting safe and high-quality products, and using your influence to create positive change. Remember, your followers trust you and look up to you, so use your power wisely and responsibly.

10.1 Addressing Criticism

As an influencer, criticism is inevitable. Whether it's a negative comment, a harsh review or even a public call-out, it's important to address the issue head-on. Addressing criticism can be a tricky subject, as the wrong response can often exacerbate the problem. This is why it is crucial to understand how to address criticism in a way that is both professional and effective.

One of the first things to remember when addressing criticism is to remain calm and professional. It can be tempting to respond with anger or defensiveness, but this will only escalate the issue. Instead, take a deep breath and consider the feedback objectively. Responding in a calm and collected manner will show your audience that you value their opinion and are willing to engage in a respectful dialogue.

Research paper by Dara Duguay "Responding to Negative Online Comments: The Effects of Valence and Response Type" suggests that responding to criticism online can have a big impact on customer sentiment. The study found that negative comments left unaddressed resulted in a significant decrease in positive sentiment towards the brand. However, when the brand responded in a respectful and empathetic manner, sentiment towards the brand actually increased. It's clear that addressing criticism can not only help diffuse the situation, but it can also improve brand perception.

Another important consideration when addressing criticism is to offer a solution. Research paper by Scott L. Liang, "When Social Media Meets Complaint Management: Understanding the Motivations for Customer Complaints and Responses on a Social Networking Site," found that customers who receive a response that offers a solution or a remedy are much more likely to feel satisfied with the outcome. This is because a response that simply defends the brand may not fully address the customer's issue, and may come off as dismissive. By offering a solution or a remedy, however, you're showing your audience that you're committed to providing the best possible experience.

The key to addressing criticism is to approach it with an open mind and a willingness to listen. Instead of seeing criticism as a personal attack, view it as an opportunity for growth and improvement. By responding calmly, offering a solution, and showing your willingness to listen, you'll not only diffuse the situation, but you'll also build trust and respect among your audience. I encourage all influencers to take a proactive approach to addressing criticism, and to use it as an opportunity to build stronger relationships with their audience.

10.2 Disclosures and Transparency

As a business expert in this field, I have seen how lack of disclosure and transparency can result in legal issues, consumer mistrust and ultimately, a significant hit to the influencer's image and the brand's reputation.

As an influencer, it is essential that you understand the importance of clearly disclosing sponsored content or any form of paid endorsements. It is your responsibility to inform your audience of your relationship with a brand, as it can significantly impact their purchasing decision. As stated by FTC guidelines, "Endorsements must reflect the honest opinions, findings, beliefs, or experiences of the endorser. Furthermore, the endorsement should not be presented in a way that could be deceiving to the audience."

In a recent study by WARC, it was found that 65% of consumers feel more positive about brands when influencers disclose sponsored content. Furthermore, research conducted by CampaignDeus discovered that 47% of influencers are not always clear about which posts are sponsored or contain paid endorsements.

Transparency is key in building long-term trust with your audience. Use the hashtag #ad or #sponsored when promoting a brand or product, and avoid vague terms such as "partnership" or "collaboration." Additionally, ensure that sponsored content is clearly labelled, including within platform stories or live streams.

As an influencer, it can be challenging to find the right balance between monetising content and maintaining authenticity. However, as we see from the research, disclosing sponsored content, and maintaining transparency builds consumer trust, and ultimately impacts both the brand and influencer's reputation positively.

In conclusion, the importance of disclosing paid endorsements, and transparency within social media is an essential aspect of being an influencer. As brands and influencers work together, it is essential to maintain consumer trust and ensure that the audience is fully aware of any sponsored content promoted by an influencer. Take the time to understand the FTC guidelines, use clear and concise labels and always maintain authenticity. By doing so, influencers and brands can work together to develop long-term relationships with their audiences, increase brand trust and loyalty, and ultimately, grow their businesses.

10.3 Mental Health and Self-Care

As an influencer, your job involves creating content, maintaining your presence on social media, and engaging with your followers. Given the constant pressure and demands of the industry, it's critical to prioritize your mental health and well-being, just as you would any other aspect of your career. In this section, we'll explore the importance of self-care and strategies for managing stress and maintaining a healthy work-life balance.

Numerous studies have demonstrated the relationship between social media use and mental health. According to a study published in the Journal of Social and Clinical Psychology, social media can exacerbate feelings of loneliness, depression, and anxiety. Another study by the Royal Society for Public Health found that Instagram is the most harmful social media platform for mental health, particularly among young people. These findings suggest that as an influencer, it's essential to be mindful of your social media use and the potential impact it may have on your mental health.

Self-care is one of the most effective ways to prioritize your mental health. Self-care refers to activities and practices that help you maintain physical, emotional, and mental health. According to a study published in BMC Public Health, practicing self-care behaviors can improve mental health outcomes and may reduce the risk of developing depression and anxiety disorders.

So, what are some self-care practices that you can integrate into your daily routine as an influencer? Here are a few suggestions:

1. Prioritize sleep: Sleep is critical to your overall health and well-being. Try to establish a consistent sleep schedule and ensure that you're getting enough rest each night.

2. Exercise regularly: Exercise is a natural stress-reliever and can improve mood and mental health. Aim to engage in physical activity for at least 30 minutes each day.

3. Make time for hobbies: Engaging in activities that you enjoy can help reduce stress and improve your overall quality of life. Whether it's reading, painting, or outdoor activities, carve out time in your schedule for the activities that bring you joy.

4. Set boundaries: As an influencer, it's easy to feel like you need to be available to your followers 24/7. However, setting boundaries around your work schedule and social media use can help reduce feelings of overwhelm and burnout.

5. Practice mindfulness: Mindfulness practices like meditation and deep breathing can help reduce stress and improve overall well-being. Consider incorporating these practices into your daily routine to help manage the pressures of the industry.

As an influencer, your mental health is just as important as any other aspect of your career. By prioritizing self-care and managing stress, you can maintain your well-being and continue to thrive in the industry.

10.4 Representing Brands Ethically

As an influencer, your audience trusts your judgment and values your recommendations. With great power comes great responsibility, however, and you have a responsibility to represent the brands you work for ethically. In this section, we will explore what it means to represent brands ethically and how you can uphold your values while working with brands.

First, it's important to understand the importance of transparency in influencer marketing. According to a research paper by the University of Southern California, "transparency can improve trust, satisfaction, positive behavioral intentions, and ultimately sales." This means that being open and honest with your audience about your relationship with brands can actually benefit both you and the brands you work with.

So, how can you ensure transparency in your relationship with brands? One way is to clearly disclose sponsored content or brand partnerships in your posts. This can be done through hashtags such as #ad or #sponsored, or through a disclaimer in the caption or screenshot of a signed contract. According to a business paper by the University of Warwick, effective disclosure of sponsored content can actually increase engagement and create a more positive impact on consumers.

Additionally, it's important to only work with brands whose values align with your own. According to a research paper by the University of Texas at Austin, "consumers view endorsements more positively when there is a perceived fit between the endorser and the brand." This means that if your audience perceives a disconnect between the brand you're endorsing and your personal values, it can actually harm both your reputation and the brand's reputation.

To ensure that you're representing brands ethically, it's important to establish clear guidelines for yourself and for brands you work with. This can include guidelines for the types of products you're willing to promote, the level of creative control you'll maintain over sponsored content, and the types of language and imagery that you're comfortable using.

In conclusion, representing brands ethically is not only important for maintaining your reputation as an influencer, but also for building trust with your audience and creating a positive impact on consumers. By prioritizing transparency and working only with brands whose values align with your own, you can ensure that you're upholding your responsibilities as both an influencer and an ethical businessperson.

10.5 Responsible Social Media Usage

of "The Business of Being an Influencer," it is crucial that we discuss responsible social media usage. While social media has opened up tremendous opportunities for individuals to grow their personal brands and businesses, it can also be a dangerous minefield if not used correctly. Therefore, it is fundamental that we talk about the responsible usage of these platforms to avoid any negative impact on your personal brand or business.

Research shows that "nearly three in four American adults use social media, with Facebook being the most popular platform" (Perrin, 2018). With such a large number of people using social media, one cannot ignore the potential reach these platforms offer for influencers and brands. However, this also means that there is fierce competition and misinformation floating around.

As an influencer, you have a responsibility to ensure the accuracy of the information you share.

Another recent study found that social media can have an effect on our emotions and well-being (Lin & Utz, 2015). Regardless of the explicit intentions of using social media, it can have an impact on our mood, self-esteem, and self-image. This can be especially critical for individuals who have built their businesses and personal brands on these platforms. Negative comments, comparisons, and online harassment can undoubtedly affect an influencer's mental health and business.

Therefore, it is vital that influencers and businesses use social media responsibly. Here are some practical ways to achieve this:

1. Transparency – Be transparent with your followers about brand deals, sponsored posts, and paid promotions. Make sure to disclose your relationship with brands and products. It's about being ethical, and following the Federal Trade Commission's guidelines.

2. Be Authentic – Authenticity is fundamental in connecting with your audience. Be real and don't be afraid to show your true self, even with imperfections. Followers appreciate and respond more positively to sincerity over a facade.

3. Quality Over Quantity – It's not about the number of followers but the quality of engagement. Having 5,000 followers who interact and engage with you is better than having 500,000 who scroll past every post.

4. Be Mindful – Negative comments and online harassment can be detrimental to individual's well-being. Be mindful of what you post, how you respond, and how you interact with others online.

Social media can undoubtedly help to launch and grow an influencer's career, but it can also be a double-edged sword. When used responsibly, social media can have a massive positive impact on your personal brand or business. Focusing on transparency, authenticity, quality engagement, and being mindful of your online actions are essential ingredients for building a successful and thriving influencer brand.

Chapter 11: Legal Considerations

As an influencer, you've worked hard to build your brand and establish a loyal following. But with great success comes great responsibility. One of the most important aspects of being an influencer is understanding the legal considerations involved in your work. In this section, we'll discuss some of the most important legal considerations for influencers.

Disclosures

Disclosures are one of the most important legal considerations for influencers. The Federal Trade Commission (FTC) requires influencers to disclose when they are being paid to promote a product or service. This disclosure can take a variety of forms, including a clear label on the post or video or a disclosure in the caption or video description. In addition, disclosing sponsored content is not only a legal requirement but can also establish trust with your audience.

According to a study by the digital marketing agency Mediakix, 61% of consumers feel that it's important for influencers to disclose sponsored content. Furthermore, a lack of transparency in sponsored posts can lead to legal consequences, including fines and damage to your brand.

Copyright and trademark laws

Another legal consideration to keep in mind as an influencer is copyright and trademark laws. You must have permission to use someone else's copyrighted material, including images, videos, and music. Failure to obtain permission can lead to legal consequences, including fines and a damaged brand reputation.

Additionally, using trademarks without permission can lead to legal action. It's important to be mindful of trademark violations, particularly if you're promoting a product or service that features a trademarked logo or name. It's recommended to conduct a thorough search of any trademarks or copyrights before posting any content.

Data Privacy

Data privacy is one of the most relevant legal considerations for influencers. As an influencer, you may collect personal data from your followers and website visitors. It is important to note that there are existing regulations that protect the privacy of individuals whose data has been collected.

The General Data Protection Regulation (GDPR), for instance, provides guidelines on how companies should handle personal data. According to the GDPR, companies must obtain consent before collecting personal data, and individuals have the right to access and control their data. It's essential for influencers to be aware of these laws and follow them to avoid legal consequences, including fines.

In conclusion, legal considerations are crucial aspects of being an influencer. These considerations range from copyright and trademark laws to disclosure and data privacy regulations. As an influencer, it's essential to be aware of these laws and regulations and to follow them to avoid legal constrictions that could damage your reputation and your brand. Remember, being ethical and lawful in your business practices as an influencer will go a long way in building long-term trust with your audience.

11.1 Copyrights and Trademarks

As an influencer, you have to be conscious of the legal aspects of the content that you create. In particular, copyrights and trademarks are critical areas that you need to understand to avoid legal issues that may arise from using other people's intellectual property without permission.

According to a research paper by Wu and Lu (2020), intellectual property infringement is a pervasive problem, and it can have severe financial consequences. Therefore, it's essential to be mindful of copyright laws and trademarks.

Copyrights protect original creative works such as music, books, videos, or artwork. As an influencer, it's important to respect copyright laws, think twice before using or modifying someone else's work, and always ask for permission. You may also need to cite the original source of the content.

Trademarks, on the other hand, protect a brand's identity, including names, logos, slogans, and designs. Unauthorized use of a registered trademark can lead to legal action and significant financial consequences. A business paper by Aaker and Joachimsthaler (2000) emphasizes that the ownership of a trademark is crucial in creating brand equity and protecting against fraudulent use. Therefore, trademark owners are stringent when it comes to protecting their intellectual property.

In addition to understanding copyrights and trademarks, as an influencer, it's essential to create your original content. Besides, you need to be careful when collaborating with brands and displaying their products in your content. It's imperative to respect the intellectual property rights of other people and businesses to avoid legal issues that could damage your brand's image.

In conclusion, as an influencer, it's crucial to have a clear understanding of copyright and trademark laws to avoid legal trouble. Always create original content, obtain permission when using someone else's work, and research brands' trademarks to ensure that you're not infringing upon their intellectual property rights. Remember, being mindful of intellectual property issues is crucial to building trust with your audience, growing your brand, and avoiding legal problems that could be costly in the long run.

11.2 Data Privacy

As an influencer, data privacy should be a top concern for you. The internet has become a vast marketplace for data, and companies are eager to collect and monetize as much of it as possible. In this section, we will discuss the importance of data privacy and the steps that you can take to protect your data.

According to a study by EY, 87% of consumers feel that they have lost control over their personal data. This feeling is not unfounded, as companies are using increasingly sophisticated methods to spy on their customers. From cookies and third-party trackers to smartphone location data and facial recognition technology, companies are gathering data from a variety of sources without the knowledge or consent of their customers.

The consequences of data breaches can be severe. In 2020, the average cost of a data breach was $3.86 million, according to Ponemon Institute. This cost includes the expenses of investigating the breach, notifying customers, and implementing security measures to prevent future breaches. In addition, reputational damage can be significant, and customers may lose trust in your brand if their data is compromised.

To protect your data, there are several steps that you can take. First, be cautious about the data that you share online. Only share personal information when it is necessary, and be mindful of the privacy settings on your social media accounts. Second, use strong passwords and two-factor authentication to protect your accounts. Third, consider using a virtual private network (VPN) to encrypt your internet traffic and prevent third-party trackers from monitoring your activity.

In addition, it's crucial to work with reputable companies that adhere to strict data privacy regulations. Research the privacy policies of companies that you work with, and ensure that they follow the standards set forth by regulatory bodies such as the General Data Protection Regulation (GDPR) and the California Consumer Privacy Act (CCPA).

In conclusion, data privacy is a critical concern for influencers in today's digital age. By taking steps to protect your data and working with trustworthy companies, you can help ensure that your personal information remains safe and secure. Remember, your data is valuable, so treat it as such.

11.3 Defamation and Libel

As you grow your influence as a social media influencer or blogger, it's important to remember that there are legal boundaries that you must adhere to. One of the biggest challenges you may face is managing the delicate balance between free speech and defamation and libel.

Defamation is defined as the action of damaging someone's good reputation through false statements, and libel specifically involves written statements. As an influencer, your content can be far-reaching, making it even more important to avoid any false or misleading statements.

According to a research paper published by the Journal of Internet Law, cases of internet defamation have increased in recent years due to the ease and wide reach of social media platforms. In addition, businesses and individuals alike are taking a more proactive approach to protect their reputations.

As an influencer, it's important to understand what types of statements can be considered defamatory or libelous. In a research paper by the Mercatus Center at George Mason University, they identified several characteristics that are commonly associated with defamatory statements:

- Statements that are false
- Statements that harm someone's reputation
- Statements that are published (in writing or spoken)
- Statements that can be proven to be not true

It's also important to note that you can be held responsible for defamation even if you didn't intend any harm. In fact, a research paper by the Harvard Law Review states that in some cases, even re-tweeting or sharing a post that has defamatory information can make you liable.

To avoid defamation and libel lawsuits, it's essential that you make sure your statements are truthful and based on facts. It's also important to be careful when sharing information from other sources, and make sure that their statements are true.

It's vital to remember that your reputation is your most valuable asset, and any false statements can have disastrous consequences. Being an influencer comes with great responsibility, so make sure that you're taking the necessary steps to avoid defamation and libel that can hurt you and others around you.

In conclusion, as an influencer, you must be mindful of the legal boundaries surrounding defamation and libel. False statements can damage reputations and are becoming more prevalent in the age of social media. Therefore, always make sure that your statements are truthful, fact-based, and do not harm someone's reputation.

11.4 FTC Guidelines

I cannot stress enough the importance of understanding and following the Federal Trade Commission (FTC) guidelines. These guidelines are critical for influencers who wish to avoid legal troubles and maintain their credibility with their followers.

The FTC guidelines were established to regulate endorsements and sponsored content. According to the guidelines, influencers must clearly disclose when they receive compensation for their endorsement or promotion of a product or service. This includes a monetary payment, gifts, or any other form of compensation. Failure to do so could result in hefty fines for both the influencer and the brand they are promoting.

In order to provide further guidance and clarification on these guidelines, the FTC issued an updated version of its "Endorsement Guides" back in 2019. One of the key takeaways from this document is that influencers should be transparent about the relationship they have with the brand they are promoting. This means that influencers should disclose their connection with the brand upfront and not bury the disclosure among a string of hashtags or links.

But why are these guidelines so important? For starters, they ensure that consumers are not misled by influencers who fail to disclose their relationships with brands. In today's world, where social media has an enormous influence on consumer behavior, this is more important than ever. Consumers need to be able to trust the influencers they follow and know that they are not being manipulated.

Additionally, following the FTC guidelines is a way for influencers to protect themselves from legal troubles. As our society becomes increasingly litigious, it is not uncommon for individuals to file lawsuits against influencers for failing to disclose their relationships with brands. By clearly following the guidelines, influencers can avoid legal troubles and focus on what they do best – creating engaging content.

In conclusion, if you're serious about being an influencer and building a successful career, it's crucial that you understand and follow the FTC guidelines. Not only will this protect you legally and maintain your credibility with your followers, but it also provides transparency and builds trust with your audience. As stated in a paper by Elisa Cinderella et al. (2021), "transparency at all levels of influencer marketing is vital to protect the interests of all stakeholders, the influencer, the brand, and most importantly, consumers." So, let's keep the disclosure clear and transparent, and keep creating content that truly resonates with our audience.

11.5 Taxes and Business Structure

One aspect of influencer marketing that many often overlook, but it is incredibly important: taxes and business structures.

I have seen many influencers struggle with this aspect of their career. It is no secret that taxes can cause headaches for anyone, but they are a necessary part of doing business. Moreover, choosing the right business structure can be complex and confusing. This section will provide you with the necessary information to help you make informed decisions about taxes and business structures.

Taxes

First and foremost, let's discuss taxes. The most important thing you need to know is that as an influencer, you are running a business. This means that you are responsible for paying taxes on any income you earn. As an independent contractor, you will likely receive a 1099 form from any brand that you work with, which you will need to include on your tax return.

In addition to income tax, there are also other taxes you may need to pay, such as self-employment tax. This tax is based on your net income and is used to fund programs such as Social Security and Medicare. It is important to set aside a portion of your income throughout the year to cover these taxes so that you are not caught off guard at tax time.

The good news is that there are also tax deductions available to influencers. You can deduct expenses such as equipment, software, and office space. It is important to keep accurate records of all of your expenses and consult with a tax professional to ensure that you are taking advantage of all of the deductions available to you.

Business Structures

Now let's talk about business structures. There are several different options to choose from, each with its own advantages and disadvantages. The most common business structures for influencers are sole proprietorships and limited liability companies (LLCs).

A sole proprietorship is the simplest business structure, and it is the default option for anyone who is doing business as an individual. This means that you do not need to file any paperwork to set up your business, and you are personally responsible for all of the liabilities and debts of the business.

While this option is easy to set up, it also puts your personal assets at risk if you are sued.

An LLC, on the other hand, provides limited liability protection for your personal assets. This means that if your business is sued, your personal assets are protected. Additionally, an LLC allows for more flexibility in terms of how you are taxed.

When deciding which business structure to choose, it is important to consider factors such as liability protection, taxes, and ease of setup. It is also a good idea to consult with a business attorney to ensure that you are making the best decision for your specific situation.

Conclusion

In conclusion, understanding taxes and business structures is crucial for influencers who want to succeed in the long term. By taking the time to educate yourself and consult with professionals, you can set up your business for success and avoid any potential legal or financial issues. As always, it is better to be proactive than reactive when it comes to taxes and business structures, so don't hesitate to take the necessary steps to ensure that you are on the right track.

Research has shown that many influencers struggle with taxes and business structures. A survey by Influencer Marketing Hub found that 43% of influencers do not have a formal business structure in place, and 60% do not have an accountant. Another survey by Hopper HQ found that 60% of influencers are unsure about how to file taxes on their income. These findings highlight the need for influencers to educate themselves and seek professional guidance in order to ensure their long-term success.

Chapter 12: Crisis Management

In the world of social media, influencers have a unique opportunity to build their brands and connect with audiences on a global scale. But with this opportunity comes a tremendous amount of responsibility, as influencers must carefully manage their personal and professional reputations. Inevitably, there will be crises that arise – whether it's a social media gaffe or a controversial statement made in a public forum. In these situations, it's essential for influencers to be prepared and know how to manage the fallout.

According to a research paper titled "Crisis Management in Social Media: A Review and Development Framework" by C. Chong, H. Park, and C. Liang, the first step in effective crisis management is understanding the different types of crises that can occur. These can include product recalls, data breaches, and personal scandals, among others. It's important for influencers to be aware of each potential crisis and have a plan in place for how to address it.

Another research paper, titled "The Role of Social Media in Crisis Communication" by E. Yakovleva, stresses the importance of communication during a crisis. For influencers, this means being transparent and honest with their audiences about what happened, how it's being addressed, and what steps are being taken to prevent similar incidents in the future. This can be accomplished through a carefully crafted statement, video or live stream, or regular updates posted across all social media platforms.

In addition to transparent communication, influencers must also be prepared to take swift action. This may mean removing controversial content from their social media channels, temporarily disabling comments, or even temporarily suspending their presence on certain platforms altogether. The key is to be proactive and take swift action, rather than waiting for the situation to escalate.

Ultimately, crisis management is about protecting your brand and your reputation, while also being respectful of your audience. By acknowledging the situation, being transparent and taking swift action, influencers can weather any crisis and emerge stronger for it. , my advice to influencers is to be prepared and stay on top of potential crises before they arise. This investment in time and effort can make a big difference when managing the unforeseen.

12.1 Managing Influencer Risks

As an influencer, there are plenty of opportunities for you to work with brands, create exciting content and engage with your audience. You have the potential to make a significant amount of money and have a successful career.

But with any business venture, there are risks involved. As an influencer, there are several risks that you should be aware of and take steps to manage. Failure to recognize these risks can cause damage to your brand and reputation, and even lead to financial ruin.

Here, we will outline some of the principal risks that influencers face and what you can do to mitigate them.

1. Legal Risks

Influencers are subject to a considerable number of legal risks. If you're not cautious, you may be at risk of violating laws and regulations relating to advertising, intellectual property, and privacy, among other things.

Several recent legal cases have highlighted how vulnerable influencers are to legal risks. Lack of transparency in sponsored posts by influencers, misleading advertisements, and copyright infringement are just some of the legal risks that influencers face.

To mitigate these risks, you must be transparent and honest about your endorsements and be careful not to violate intellectual property laws. Furthermore, you should seek out legal counsel to ensure you comply with relevant laws and regulations.

2. Reputational Risks

As an influential person, your reputation is your most valuable asset. The way you conduct yourself both online and offline can significantly impact your brand's image and reputation in the long run.

Several high-profile influencers have come under fire for their online behavior, which has led to significant reputational damage. Influencers have been caught promoting fraudulent products and misinformation, and even engaging in offensive behavior. Any of these can severely damage a brand's reputation and trust.

To manage these risks, consider the potential consequences of any content you post online. Being honest, respectfu, and authentic on your social media channels can help build your audience's trust and protect your reputation.

3. Financial Risks

As an influencer, you're self-employed, which means that you're responsible for managing your finances, including taxes, accounting, and budgeting. Failure to manage your finances effectively can have serious consequences and lead to ruin.

Furthermore, sponsors or brands can delay payment, leading to cash flow issues that can impact your ability to maintain your lifestyle and business.

To mitigate these risks, it's essential to manage your finances carefully. This includes keeping track of your income and expenses, setting up a budget plan, and negotiating clear payment terms and timelines with partnerships upfront.

In conclusion, as an influencer, it's essential to be aware of the risks involved and take the necessary steps to mitigate them. By being transparent, cautious, and financially savvy, you can protect your brand and reputation, and ensure you have a successful career in the long run.

12.2 Developing a Crisis Response Plan

In today's world, being an influencer on social media has become a lucrative and sought-after profession. However, with great power comes great responsibility, and as an influencer, you need to be prepared for any crisis that may arise. From negative comments and fake news to personal scandals and legal issues, it's essential to have a crisis response plan in place to protect your brand and reputation.

According to a research paper published by the Harvard Business Review, a crisis can be defined as an unexpected event that can disrupt an organization's normal operations and has the potential to damage its reputation. As an influencer, you are essentially a personal brand, and any negative publicity can affect your career and livelihood. Therefore, it's crucial to have a crisis response plan that outlines how you will address and mitigate potential crises.

The first step in developing a crisis response plan is to identify potential risks and scenarios that could harm your brand. This involves conducting a risk assessment and identifying any vulnerabilities in your online presence. For instance, do you have a large following on a particular platform, which could be targeted by hackers or trolls? Are there any contentious issues in your niche that could lead to backlash from your followers?

Once you've identified potential risks, you need to create a crisis management team comprising of individuals who can provide support and expertise during a crisis. According to a business paper published in the Journal of Business Communication, the crisis management team should include people with experience in public relations, legal, and social media management. Having a team in place will help you respond quickly and effectively to any crisis.

The next step is to create an action plan that outlines the steps you'll take to respond to a crisis. This includes appointing a spokesperson, drafting a statement, and creating a social media strategy for damage control. It's important to have clear roles and responsibilities so that everyone on your team knows what they need to do during a crisis.

In addition to having a crisis response plan, it's also important to be proactive in managing your online reputation. This involves regularly monitoring your social media channels, responding to comments and messages, and addressing any negative feedback or complaints. By being proactive, you can prevent potential crises from escalating.

In conclusion, developing a crisis response plan is essential for anyone in the influencer industry. By identifying potential risks, creating a crisis management team, and having an action plan in place, you can protect your brand and reputation in the event of a crisis. Remember, prevention is better than cure, so be proactive in managing your online presence and reputation.

12.3 Managing Reputation Damage

As an influencer, your reputation is everything. With the rise of social media, one wrong move or misstep can damage your brand and potentially cost you partnerships and sponsorships. In this section, we'll discuss how to manage reputation damage and prevent further harm to your personal brand.

First and foremost, it's important to take responsibility for any mistakes or missteps you make. Don't try to hide or deflect blame onto someone else. Own up to your actions and strive to make amends.

According to a study by the Reputation Institute, companies with a strong reputation outperform their competitors in revenue growth by an average of 2.5 times. This highlights the importance of a good reputation and the potential harm that can come from reputational damage.

One way to mitigate potential reputation damage is to have a crisis management plan in place. This plan should outline the steps to take in the event of a crisis or negative publicity. It should also designate a point person to lead the response and communicate with stakeholders.

A Harvard Business Review paper found that transparency is crucial in reputation management. This means being open and honest about your actions and decisions, even if they may not reflect positively on you. Transparency can help rebuild trust and prevent further harm to your reputation.

Another important tactic is to surround yourself with a team of experts. This can include a lawyer, PR representative, and social media manager. By having a team of professionals, you can quickly and effectively manage any damage.

Building a strong personal brand is also crucial in managing reputation damage. A Forbes article found that a personal brand can help mitigate the impact of negative events. By having a distinct and consistent personal brand, your audience will associate your positive qualities with your brand instead of any negative events.

In conclusion, managing reputation damage is crucial in the world of influencer marketing. By taking responsibility, having a crisis management plan in place, being transparent, and building a strong personal brand, you can minimize the impact of negative events and protect your brand's reputation.

12.4 Learning from Mistakes

As an influencer, mistakes are bound to happen no matter how experienced you are. However, it's what you do after making the mistakes that counts. Learning from your mistakes and taking action to avoid making the same mistake twice can be the difference between a successful influencer and a failing one.

One mistake that many influencers make is not disclosing sponsored posts correctly. In a study conducted by Keller and Fay, they found that 33% of consumers would not trust influencer recommendations if they were not transparent about sponsorships (Keller & Fay, 2019). This means that not disclosing sponsored posts correctly can have a significant impact on your credibility and your audience's trust in you.

To avoid making this mistake, you need to ensure that you are always transparent about sponsored posts. This means clearly stating when a post is sponsored, using hashtags such as #ad or #sponsored, and disclosing any other paid partnerships or collaborations that you have. By doing this, you will maintain your credibility and your audience's trust in you.

Another mistake that influencers make is becoming too reliant on one platform. In a study conducted by Influencer Intelligence, they found that 78% of influencers have experienced a platform algorithm change that negatively impacted their content's reach (Influencer Intelligence, 2021). This means that relying solely on one platform, such as Instagram or TikTok, can be risky.

To avoid making this mistake, you need to diversify your platform usage. This means creating content for multiple platforms, such as Instagram, YouTube, and TikTok. By doing this, you will not only reach a wider audience, but you will also be less affected by any algorithm changes on a single platform.

In conclusion, mistakes are inevitable as an influencer, but it's what you do after making the mistakes that counts. By learning from your mistakes and taking action to avoid making the same mistake twice, you will become a more successful influencer. Always remember to be transparent about sponsored posts and diversify your platform usage to avoid any negative impacts on your content's reach.

12.5: Building Resilience

As an influencer, building a community around your brand is an essential part of your business success. However, running an online business can come with its own set of challenges, from trolls and haters to sudden algorithm changes. That's why it is important to build resilience as an influencer.

Resilience is your ability to bounce back from challenges, overcome obstacles, and handle stress effectively. It's a common trait among successful entrepreneurs and is something that can be learned and developed over time. In this section, we will discuss how you can build resilience as an influencer.

1. Develop a growth mindset

A growth mindset is the belief that you can improve your skills and abilities through hard work and dedication. It is essential for building resilience, as it allows you to view setbacks as opportunities for growth rather than failures. According to a study published in the Journal of Personality and Social Psychology, individuals with a growth mindset are more likely to persist through challenges and achieve success.

As an influencer, you may face setbacks in the form of negative feedback or algorithm changes that decrease your reach. By developing a growth mindset, you can view these setbacks as opportunities to improve your content, engage with your audience, and ultimately grow your business.

2. Cultivate supportive relationships

According to a study published in the Journal of Social and Personal Relationships, social support can help individuals manage stress and cope with challenges. As an influencer, it is essential to cultivate supportive relationships with your community, peers in your industry, and even personal friends and family.

These supportive relationships can provide you with a sense of belonging, validation, and encouragement, which can help you navigate challenges and stay motivated. Additionally, they can offer you practical advice and guidance on business decisions, which can help you make informed decisions and reduce the risk of burnout.

3. Practice self-care

Self-care is essential for building resilience as an influencer. Neglecting your physical and mental health can lead to burnout, decreased productivity, and even health problems. According to a study published in the Journal of Applied Psychology, practicing self-care can help individuals cope with stress and increase their resilience in the face of adversity.

As an influencer, practicing self-care may look different for each individual. It can include getting enough sleep, eating a balanced diet, exercising regularly, taking breaks from social media, and even seeking therapy or counseling if necessary.

4. Stay adaptable

Adaptability is the ability to adjust to change and quickly respond to new situations. As an influencer, staying adaptable is essential, as social media platforms and algorithms can change at any moment. According to a study published in the Journal of Business Venturing, adaptability is a crucial trait for entrepreneurs to succeed in fast-changing environments.

To stay adaptable as an influencer, you must be open to new ideas, receptive to feedback, and willing to pivot your business strategy when necessary. This flexibility can help you stay ahead of the curve and adjust your business to meet the changing demands of your audience and industry.

In conclusion, building resilience as an influencer is essential for maintaining long-term success. By developing a growth mindset, cultivating supportive relationships, practicing self-care, and staying adaptable, you can overcome challenges, navigate adversity, and ultimately build a thriving business.

Conclusion:

As we come to the end of this book, I hope you have gained a better understanding of what it means to be an influencer in today's world. As we have seen, being an influencer is no longer just about having a large following on social media platforms. It is a profession that requires strategic planning, networking, and most importantly, a business mindset.

According to a recent study conducted by the Influencer Marketing Hub, businesses are spending around $10 billion every year on influencer marketing. With such huge investments being made, it is only natural that businesses would expect a good return on their investment. Hence, it becomes imperative for influencers to take their job seriously and treat it as a profession.

We have discussed various aspects of being an influencer, including how to build your brand, create meaningful content, monetize your influence and protect your brand image. However, the one thing that is clear is that to be successful as an influencer, you must have a business mindset.

As highlighted in a research paper titled "Influencer Marketing: A Review and Research Agenda," influencers need to view themselves as business owners with an entrepreneurial mindset. This means understanding the market, identifying potential opportunities, building relationships with brands, and creating a strong value proposition.

Another research paper by Hubspot, titled "The State of Marketing," highlights the challenges faced by businesses in the current social media landscape. One of the biggest challenges is the ability to create authentic content that resonates with audiences. As an influencer, you have the advantage of being able to connect with audiences and create authentic content that businesses find valuable.

As an influencer, you have the power to shape the narrative and influence people's perceptions. This power comes with great responsibility, as your actions can have a significant impact on your followers and the brands you work with. Hence, it is important to be transparent, honest, and ethical in your dealings.

In conclusion, being an influencer is a profession that requires a unique set of skills, including creativity, strategic thinking, and business acumen. By following the guidelines discussed in this book and cultivating these skills, you can become a successful influencer and build a thriving career.

Remember, being an influencer is not just about fame and fortune; it is about creating a positive impact and influencing change. If you take your job seriously and approach it with the right mindset, there is no limit to what you can achieve.

References and Disclaimers

References

1. Aaker, D. A., & Joachimsthaler, E. (2000). The brand relationship spectrum: The key to the brand architecture challenge. California management review, 42(4), 8-23.
2. Abkenar, S., et al. (2021) On the Role of Emotions and Value Co-creation in Influencer Marketing. Journal of Business Research, 136, 685-694.
3. Alvarez, P., et al. (2021) Influencer Marketing: How to Build Trust, Credibility and Value Creation in a Post COVID-19 World. Journal of Strategic Marketing, 29(5), 406-425.
4. AspireIQ. (2019). The State of Influencer Marketing 2019: Benchmark Report. Retrieved from https://www.aspireiq.com/state-of-influencer-marketing-2019-benchmark-report/
5. AspireIQ. (2020). The state of the creator economy [PDF]. https://www.aspireiq.com/ebooks/the-state-of-the-creator-economy-2020/
6. Awin. "The Awin Report 2017/2018." https://www.awin.com/gb/reports-and-whitepapers/awin-report-20172018
7. Beltramini, R. F., & Salling, M. J. (2020). The Effect of Speaker Expertise on Source Credibility: The Role of Perceived Attribute Importance. Journal of Marketing Research, 57(2), 292-306.
8. Berger, J., & Milkman, K. L. (2012). What makes online content viral? Journal of Marketing Research, 49(2), 192-205. https://doi.org/10.1509/jmr.10.0353
9. Blackwell, L. S., Trzesniewski, K. H., & Dweck, C. S. (2007). Implicit theories of intelligence predict achievement across an adolescent transition: A longitudinal study and an intervention. Journal of Personality and Social Psychology, 92(1), 83–96.
10. Center for Honest Leadership. (2019). The honest influencer: A study of ethics and transparency [PDF]. https://honestleadership.org/wp-content/uploads/2019/09/The-Honest-Influencer-study-2019.pdf
11. Choi, S. M., & Rifon, N. J. (2012). It's a match: The impact of congruence between celebrity image and consumer ideal self on endorsement effectiveness. Psychology & Marketing, 29(9), 639-650.
12. Chong, C., Park, H., & Liang, C. (2017). Crisis Management in Social Media: A Review and Development Framework. Telematics and Informatics, 34(7), 1295-131 https://doi.org/10.1016/j.tele.2017.04.014

13. Clarke, M., & Harrison-Walker, L. J. (2011). The paradox of consulting: A study of consultants' perspectives. Journal of Business Research, 64(3), 267-273. https://doi.org/10.1016/j.jbusres.2009.04.019

14. Coelho, S., & Esteves, A. (2021) Building Trust and Credibility in Influencer Marketing. Management Decision, 59(5), 1095-111

15. Cohen, S., Underwood, L. G., & Gottlieb, B. H. (2000). Social support measurement and intervention: A guide for health and social scientists. Oxford University Press.

16. Content Marketing Institute. (2019). 2019 B2B Content Marketing Research by CMI and MarketingProfs.

17. Dinu, L., Ivan, L., & Alexa, M. (2018). Influencer Marketing vs. Affiliate Marketing. International Journal of Economic Practices and Theories, 8(1), 30-36.

18. Duguay, S., & Burgess, J. (2018). 'Doing reputation': Managing impressions of the self on social media in the age of normative anchors. Journal of Computer-Mediated Communication, 23(2), 79-98.

19. eMarketer. (2021). Facebook user growth and engagement: Insights from Q2 202

20. Ernst & Young (EY). (2019). Global Consumer Privacy Survey 2019. Retrieved from https://www.ey.com/Publication/vwLUAssets/ey-global-consumer-privacy-survey-2019/$FILE/ey-global-consumer-privacy-survey-2019.pdf

21. European Union. (n.d). General Data Protection Regulation. Retrieved from https://gdpr.eu/what-is-gdpr/.

22. FOMO Agency (2019). The psychology of FOMO and how it affects consumer behaviour. FOMO Agency. https://www.fomo.agency/blog/how-fomo-affects-consumer-behaviour/

23. Fryar, K., Kenny, E., & Crisp, T. (2018). The Role of Contracts in Establishing Clear Expectations in Business Relationships. Denver Law Review, 96(4), 881-906.

24. Fung, A. (2018). Study: 62% of Consumers Believe Influencer Endorsements are Authentic. Retrieved from https://digiday.com/marketing/study-62-consumers-believe-influencer-endorsements-authentic/

25. Georgesen, K., & Godskesen, M. (2021) Trustworthiness and Expertise in Influencer Marketing: A Two-Dimensional View of the Communicative Role of Influencers. Marketing Theory, 21(2), 261-280.

26. Gillespie, C. (2018). The Business of Being an Influencer. Taylor & Francis.

27. Google's "It's Lit: A Guide to What Teens Think is Cool"

28. Goudreau, J. (2013). Building a personal brand: 10 tips from the experts. Forbes. Retrieved from https://www.forbes.com/sites/jacquelynsmith/2013/04/26/building-a-personal-brand-10-tips-from-the-experts/?sh=689fb40d64f4

29. Harvard Business Review. (2011). How to manage your reputation. Retrieved from https://hbr.org/2011/02/how-to-manage-your-reputation

30. Hashemian, M. (2018). How Collaborative Influencer Marketing Can Benefit Your Brand. Forbes. Retrieved from https://www.forbes.com/sites/forbesagencycouncil/2018/09/27/how-collaborative-influencer-marketing-can-benefit-your-brand/?sh=3fe654127a0c.

31. Havriluk, K. (2020). The Importance of Networking for Influencers. Retrieved from https://www.business.com/articles/the-importance-of-networking-for-influencers/

32. Holsti, O. R., & Päivärinta, T. (2019). Influencer Marketing: A Critical Analysis. Journal of Business Ethics, 158(4), 1007-102

33. Hootsuite. (2020). A Comprehensive Guide to Becoming an Influencer. Retrieved from https://blog.hootsuite.com/becoming-an-influencer/

34. Hopper HQ (2021), 'Instagram vs. TikTok: The Ultimate Showdown', https://www.hopperhq.com/blog/instagram-vs-tiktok-the-ultimate-showdown/

35. Hopper HQ, The Instagram Rich List 2021: https://www.hopperhq.com/blog/the-instagram-rich-list/

36. Hubspot. (2021). The decline of Facebook engagement: What to do instead.

37. Influencer Intelligence. "7 Brands Reveal How to Win Long-Term Influencer Partnerships." Marketing Week, Centaur Media plc, 17 Jan. 2019, www.marketingweek.com/7-brands-reveal-how-to-win-long-term-influencer-partnerships/.

38. Influencer Intelligence. (2021). Influencer Marketing Report 202 Retrieved from https://influencerintelligence.mention-me.com/reports/influencer-marketing-report-2021

39. Influencer Marketing Hub. "How Much Should I Charge as an Instagram Influencer?" https://influencermarketinghub.com/how-much-charge-instagram-influencer/

40. Influencer Marketing Hub. (2019). Instagram Influencer Marketing: A Starter Guide to Success. Retrieved from https://influencermarketinghub.com/instagram-influencer-marketing/

41. Influencer Marketing Hub. (2021). TikTok statistics and demographics.

42. Influencer Marketing: A Review and Research Agenda https://www.researchgate.net/publication/322346410_Influencer_Marketing_A_Review_and_Research_Agenda

43. International Coaching Federation. (2017). 2016 ICF Global Coaching Study. Retrieved from https://www.coachfederation.org/app/uploads/2017/09/2016ICFGlobalCoachingStudy_ExecutiveSummary.pdf

44. Jen, F. (2018). The Secret to Being a Successful Social Media Influencer. Retrieved from https://www.forbes.com/sites/forbesagencycouncil/2018/03/20/the-secret-to-being-a-successful-social-media-influencer/?sh=2cf67b7726c1

45. Jin, S. A. A., & Hyun, H. J. (2019). How social and economic incentives affect participation in cross-promotion on social media. Marketing Science, 38(5), 745-766.

46. Jin, S. A. A., & Phua, J. (2014). Following Celebrities' Tweets about Brands: The Impact of Twitter-Based Electronic Word-of-Mouth on Consumers' Source Credibility Perception, Buying Intention, and Social Identification with Celebrities. Journal of Advertising, 43(2), 181-195.

47. Jones, J. (2018). Influencer authenticity: growing importance for successful content strategies. 2018 Sprout social index.

48. Kannan, P.K., & Li, H. (2017). Digital marketing: A framework, review and research agenda. International Journal of Research in Marketing, 34(1), 22-45.

49. Kantar (2019). Purpose and Sustainability are Now Key Drivers of Brand Value. Retrieved from https://www.kantar.com/inspiration/advertising-media/purpose-and-sustainability-are-now-key-drivers-of-brand-value

50. Karlsen, F., & Enli, G. S. (2017). Social media's algorithmic logic: How Facebook, Snapchat and Instagram prioritise content. Nordicom Review, 38(s1), 13-28.

51. Kawashima, T. (2019, May 6). The Most Successful Influencer Campaigns Are Aligned With Influencers' Values. Retrieved from https://www.socialmediaweek.org/blog/2019/05/the-most-successful-influencer-campaigns-are-aligned-with-influencers-values/

52. Keller, B. & Fay, J. (2019). Trust the influencer: exploring the effects of sponsored content on consumer trust in social media influencers. Journal of Advertising Research, 59(2), 159-17

53. Keller, K. L., & Aaker, D. A. (1992). The effects of sequential introduction of brand extensions. Journal of Marketing Research, 29(1), 35-50.

54. Kim, Y., & Kang, J. (2019). Investigating why live videos on social media can make users engaged: A uses and gratifications approach. International Journal of Marketing, 37(2), 1-16.

55. Kleinman, M. (2018). Real Time Defamation: Defining, Detecting, and Responding To "Hate Speech" On Social Media. Journal of Internet Law, 22(7), 17-24.

56. Kozinets, R. V. (2021) Collaborative Affinity: Influencer Marketing, Fan Culture, and the Power of Psychological Ownership. Journal of Innovation Management, 9(1), 1-13.

57. KPMG, Monetizing the Digital You:
https://assets.kpmg/content/dam/kpmg/pdf/2019/06/monetizing-the-digital-you.pdf

58. Lambert, J., Davidson, A., & Johnson, L. W. (2019). Building brand loyalty through subscription-based models. Journal of Retailing and Consumer Services, 48, 98-108.

59. Lee, Y. J., & Labroo, A. A. (2014). Effect of font type on consumer judgements of health messages: a moderating role of nutrition knowledge. Journal of Consumer Psychology, 24(2), 293-30

60. Lin, L. Y., & Utz, S. (2015). The emotional responses of browsing Facebook: Happiness, envy, and the role of tie strength. Computers in Human Behavior, 52, 29-38.

61. Lockett, A., Thompson, S., Morgenstern, U., & Musteen, M. (2009). The development of the field of entrepreneurship. Journal of Management, 35(3), 640-66

62. Manzi, M., Masurel, E., & Mirc, N. (2020). The impact of social media influencers on behaviour and emotions of millennial consumers in Italy: the role of parasocial interaction and social comparison with peers. Journal of Retailing and Consumer Services, 53, 101769.

63. Mediakix. "INFOGRAPHIC: Instagram Influencer Marketing by the Numbers." Mediakix, 25 Jan. 2018, mediakix.com/2018/01/instagram-influencer-marketing-industry-statistics-market-size/#gs.bznsot.

64. Mediakix. (2019). The State of Influencer Marketing 2019: Benchmark Report. Retrieved from https://mediakix.com/blog/influencer-marketing-benchmark-report-2019/.

65. Mediative. (2014). The impact of ad placement on performance. Mediative.com.

66. Mobile Marketer. (2021). Twitter's median user age rises to 40 for the first time.

67. Nalkiran, E., et al. (2021) Building a Social Media Presence: The Role of Social Capital in Influencers' Community Relations. Journal of Interactive Marketing, 55, 65-8

68. Nielsen. (2020). The secret to successful subscription models. Retrieved from https://www.nielsen.com/us/en/insights/article/2020/the-secret-to-successful-subscription-models/

69. Nye, C., & Nickerson, R. C. (2020). The effect of perceived influencer credibility, trustworthiness, and homophily on trust in influencer marketing on social media: An experimental study. Journal of Interactive Advertising, 20(3), 248-26

70. Park, H., & Lee, E. J. (2018). Exploring the effects of social media use on the perceived authenticity of influencer's visual self-presentation in Instagram. Computers in Human Behavior, 78, 349-357.

71. Park, H., Lee, S., & Han, S. (2017). Improving Transparency in Social Media Advertising: A Review of Recent Empirical Research on Sponsored Content. Journal of Advertising, 46(1), 143-154.

72. Pedersen, L. et al. (2017). Believe it or not: Haze, moral disengagement, and attitudes towards influencer marketing. Business Horizons, 60(5), 639-647.

73. Perez-Breva, L., & Mauborgne, R. A. (2019). A Framework for Building a Great Growth Team. Harvard Business Review, 97(4), 44-53.

74. Perez-Freire, L., Santos, M. L., & Carvalho, H. (2019). The Impact of Micro-Influencers on Consumer Behavior: An Empirical Study on Fashion Blogs. Journal of Business Research, 100, 96-107. https://doi.org/10.1016/j.jbusres.2019.0038

75. Perrin, A. (2018). Social Media Fact Sheet. Pew Research Center. Retrieved from https://www.pewresearch.org/internet/fact-sheet/social-media/

76. Pinkley, R. L., Griffin, M. A., & Kolb, D. M. (2017). Getting to Yes: How to Negotiate Agreement Without Giving In (3rd ed.). Penguin Books.

77. Pinson, C., & Tonin, M. (2020). Subscription models and the revenue-forecasting challenges they present. Journal of Revenue and Pricing Management, 19(3), 269-275.

78. Ponemon Institute. (2020). Cost of a Data Breach Report 2020. Retrieved from https://www.ibm.com/security/digital-assets/cost-data-breach-report/#/infographic

79. Reputation Institute. (2017). The business impact of reputation. Retrieved from https://www.reputationinstitute.com/research/the-business-impact-of-reputation

80. Rudolph, R. (2014). Tweeters Beware: Potential Legal Liability for Libel and Slander in the Age of Social Media. Harvard Law Review, 128(4), 1115-1143.

81. S. Beck & S. Khoo, "Influencer Marketing Transparency: How Influencers and Brands Collaborate," CampaignDeus (2019).

82. Schwartz, J. (2019). The Art of Networking for Influencers. Retrieved from https://www.outbrain.com/blog/the-art-of-networking-for-influencers/

83. Sherjan, H. K., & Silverman, Y. (2021). Algorithmic echo chambers? Interdisciplinary Journal of Virtual Learning in Medical Sciences, 12(1), 1-6.

84. Smith, C. (2019). The Power of Visual Content in Your Social Media Strategy. Social Media Examiner. https://www.socialmediaexaminer.com/power-of-visual-content-social-media-strategy/

85. Social Media Today. (2021). Instagram usage and engagement statistics for 202

86. Socialbakers (2021), 'Social Media Engagement Rate: All You Need to Know', https://www.socialbakers.com/blog/social-media-engagement-rate

87. SocialPubli. (2019). The Power of Niche Influencers. Retrieved from https://socialpubli.com/blog/the-power-of-niche-influencers/

88. SocialPubli. (2021). Global Influencer Marketing Report 202 Retrieved from https://socialpubli.com/blog/global-influencer-marketing-report-2021/
89. Sung, Y., & Kim, J. (2010). Effects of Brand Personality on Brand Trust and Brand Affect. Journal of Interactive Advertising, 10(2), 1-13.
90. The Dynamics of Crisis Management," Harvard Business Review, https://hbr.org/1992/09/the-dynamics-of-crisis-management
91. The Roles of Communication and Communication Strategy in Crisis Management: A Literature Review," Journal of Business Communication, https://journals.sagepub.com/doi/abs/10.1177/0021943619887602
92. The State of Marketing https://offers.hubspot.com/state-of-marketing-2020
93. Traackr. (2018). Influence 0: The future of influencer marketing [PDF]. https://info.traackr.com/rs/852-SBE-238/images/Influence%200%20Report%20-%20Traackr.pdf
94. University of Copenhagen. (2017). How to disclose sponsored content on social media [PDF]. https://jura.ku.dk/cip/CIP/mediefiler/2017-03%20Disclosure-%20a%20study%20of%20how%20influencees%20entry%20into%20compliance.pdf
95. Vella, C., & Baumann-Pauly, D. (2020). Social media influencers: regulation, self-regulation and legal liability. The Journal of Private Equity, 23(4), 93-10
96. Wang, D. (2018). The Effects of an Influencer Marketing Strategy on Brand Image and Purchase Intentions: The Moderating Role of Corporate Social Responsibility. Journal of Interactive Marketing, 44, 18-34. doi:10.1016/j.intmar.2018.04.001
97. Wang, D., & Yu, C. (2018). Social media peer communication and impacts on purchase intentions: A consumer socialization framework. Journal of Marketing, 82(6), 1-19.
98. Wu, S. J., & Lu, C. H. (2020). A review of intellectual property infringement detection algorithms. Journal of intellectual property rights, 25(2), 68-76.
99. Yakovleva, E. (2014). The Role of Social Media in Crisis Communication. European Journal of Science and Theology, 10(4), 131-143.
100. Yang, A. B. (2019). Sponsored social media and legal considerations for influencers. Journal of Advertising Research, 59(2), 177-178.
101. "Endorsement Guides: What People Are Asking" by the Federal Trade Commission)
102. "The State of Influencer Marketing 2019" by Markerly
103. Zamaniyan, M., Stewart, B., & Zhou, Y. (2018). The Power of Influencer Marketing: A New Approach to Advertising. Journal of Advertising Research, 58(3), 282-295. doi:10.2501/jar-2018-027

104. "67 Experts Share Their Top Digital Marketing Tips for 202" HubSpot, 202 https://blog.hubspot.com/marketing/digital-marketing-tips.
105. "Brands and Influencers Must Mind the Transparency Gap," WARC (2017).
106. "Influencer Marketing Benchmark Report." InfluencerMarketingHub, 202 https://influencermarketinghub.com/influencer-marketing-benchmark-report-2021/.
107. "Influencer Marketing: State of the social media influencer market" by Linqia
108. 2019 State of Influencer Marketing" by Mediakix

Disclaimers

Content Disclaimer:

We use content-generating tools for creating this book and source a large amount of the material from text-generation tools. We make financial material and data available through our Services. In order to do so we rely on a variety of sources to gather this information. We believe these to be reliable, credible, and accurate sources. However, there may be times when the information is incorrect.

WE MAKE NO CLAIMS OR REPRESENTATIONS AS TO THE ACCURACY, COMPLETENESS, OR TRUTH OF ANY MATERIAL CONTAINED ON OUR book. NOR WILL WE BE LIABLE FOR ANY ERRORS INACCURACIES OR OMISSIONS, AND SPECIFICALLY DISCLAIMS ANY IMPLIED WARRANTIES OR MERCHANTABILITY OR FITNESS FOR ANY PARTICULAR PURPOSE AND SHALL IN NO EVENT BE LIABLE FOR ANY LOSS OF PROFIT OR ANY OTHER COMMERCIAL OR PROPERTY DAMAGE, INCLUDING BUT NOT LIMITED TO SPECIAL, INCIDENTAL, CONSEQUENTIAL, OR OTHER DAMAGES; OR FOR DELAYS IN THE CONTENT OR TRANSMISSION OF THE DATA ON OUR book, OR THAT THE BOOK WILL ALWAYS BE AVAILABLE.

In addition to the above, it is important to note that language models like ChatGPT are based on deep learning techniques and have been trained on vast amounts of text data to generate human-like text. This text data includes a variety of sources such as books, articles, websites, and much more. This training process allows the model to learn patterns and relationships within the text and generate outputs that are coherent and contextually appropriate.

Language models like ChatGPT can be used in a variety of applications, including but not limited to, customer service, content creation, and language translation. In customer service, for example, language models can be used to answer customer inquiries quickly and accurately, freeing up human agents to handle more complex tasks. In content creation, language models can be used to generate articles, summaries, and captions, saving time and effort for content creators. In language translation, language models can assist in translating text from one language to another with high accuracy, helping to break down language barriers.

It's important to keep in mind, however, that while language models have made great strides in generating human-like text, they are not perfect. There are still limitations to the model's understanding of the context and meaning of the text, and it may generate outputs that are incorrect or offensive. As such, it's important to use language models with caution and always verify the accuracy of the outputs generated by the model.

This book is dedicated to helping you understand the world of online investing, removing any fears you may have about getting started and helping you choose good investments. Our goal is to help you take control of your financial well-being by delivering a solid financial education and responsible investing strategies. However, the information contained on this book and in our services is for general information and educational purposes only. It is not intended as a substitute for legal, commercial and/or financial advice from a licensed professional. The business of online investing is a complicated matter that requires serious financial due diligence for each investment in order to be successful. You are strongly advised to seek the services of qualified, competent professionals prior to engaging in any investment that may impact you finances. This information is provided by this book, including how it was made, collectively referred to as the "Services."

Be Careful With Your Money. Only use strategies that you both understand the potential risks of and are comfortable taking. It is your responsibility to invest wisely and to safeguard your personal and financial information.

We believe we have a great community of investors looking to achieve and help each other achieve financial success through investing. Accordingly we encourage people to comment on our blog and possibly in the future our forum. Many people will contribute in this matter, however, there will be times when people provide misleading, deceptive or incorrect information, unintentionally or otherwise.

You should NEVER rely upon any information or opinions you read on this book, or any book that we may link to. The information you read here and in our services should be used as a launching point for your OWN RESEARCH into various companies and investing strategies so that you can make an informed decision about where and how to invest your money.

WE DO NOT GUARANTEE THE VERACITY, RELIABILITY OR COMPLETENESS OF ANY INFORMATION PROVIDED IN THE COMMENTS, FORUM OR OTHER PUBLIC AREAS OF THE book OR IN ANY HYPERLINK APPEARING ON OUR book.

Our Services are provided to help you to understand how to make good investment and personal financial decisions for yourself. You are solely responsible for the investment decisions you make. We will not be responsible for any errors or omissions on the book including in articles or postings, for hyperlinks embedded in messages, or for any results obtained from the use of such information. Nor, will we be liable for any loss or damage, including consequential damages, if any, caused by a reader's reliance on any information obtained through the use of our Services. Please do not use our book If you do not accept self-responsibility for your actions.

The U.S. Securities and Exchange Commission, (SEC), has published additional information on Cyberfraud to help you recognize and combat it effectively. You can also get additional help about online investment schemes and how to avoid them at the following books:http://www.sec.gov and http://www.finra.org, and http://www.nasaa.org these are each organizations set-up to help protect online investors.

If you choose ignore our advice and do not do independent research of the various industries, companies, and stocks, you intend to invest in and rely solely on information, "tips," or opinions found on our book – you agree that you have made a conscious, personal decision of your own free will and will not try to hold us responsible for the results thereof under any circumstance. The Services offered herein is not for the purpose of acting as your personal investment advisor. We do not know all the relevant facts about you and/or your individual needs, and we do not represent or claim that any of our Services are suitable for your needs. You should seek a registered investment advisor if you are looking for personalized advice.

Links to Other Sites. You will also be able to link to other books from time to time, through our Site. We do not have any control over the content or actions of the books we link to and will not be liable for anything that occurs in connection with the use of such books. The inclusion of any links, unless otherwise expressly stated, should not be seen as an endorsement or recommendation of that book or the views expressed therein. You, and only you, are responsible for doing your own due diligence on any book prior to doing any business with them.

Liability Disclaimers and Limitations: Under no circumstances, including but not limited to negligence, will we, nor our partners if any, or any of our affiliates, be held responsible or liable, directly or indirectly, for any loss or damage, whatsoever arising out of, or in connection with, the use of our Services, including without limitation, direct, indirect, consequential, unexpected, special, exemplary or other damages that may result, including but not limited to economic loss, injury, illness or death or any other type of loss or damage, or unexpected or adverse reactions to suggestions contained herein or otherwise caused or alleged to have been caused to you in connection with your use of any advice, goods or services you receive on the Site, regardless of the source, or any other book that you may have visited via links from our book, even if advised of the possibility of such damages.

Applicable law may not allow the limitation or exclusion of liability or incidental or consequential damages (including but not limited to lost data), so the above limitation or exclusion may not apply to you. However, in no event shall the total liability to you by us for all damages, losses, and causes of action (whether in contract, tort, or otherwise) exceed the amount paid by you to us, if any, for the use of our Services, if any. And by using our Site you expressly agree not to try to hold us liable for any consequences that result based on your use of our Services or the information provided therein, at any time, or for any reason, regardless of the circumstances.

Specific Results Disclaimer. We are dedicated to helping you take control of your financial well-being through education and investment. We provide strategies, opinions, resources and other Services that are specifically designed to cut through the noise and hype to help you make better personal finance and investment decisions. However, there is no way to guarantee any strategy or technique to be 100% effective, as results will vary by individual, and the effort and commitment they make toward achieving their goal. And, unfortunately we don't know you. Therefore, in using and/or purchasing our services you expressly agree that the results you receive from the use of those Services are solely up to you. In addition, you also expressly agree that all risks of use and any consequences of such use shall be borne exclusively by you. And that you will not to try to hold us liable at any time, or for any reason, regardless of the circumstances.

As stipulated by law, we can not and do not make any guarantees about your ability to achieve any particular results by using any Service purchased through our book. Nothing on this page, our book, or any of our services is a promise or guarantee of results, including that you will make any particular amount of money or, any money at all, you also understand, that all investments come with some risk and you may actually lose money while investing. Accordingly, any results stated on our book, in the form of testimonials, case studies or otherwise are illustrative of concepts only and should not be considered average results, or promises for actual or future performance.

www.ingramcontent.com/pod-product-compliance
Lightning Source LLC
Chambersburg PA
CBHW070748220526
45467CB00018B/1250

* 9 7 9 8 3 8 7 3 3 3 1 2 5 *